The Teenage Book of Manners... PLEASE!

Fred Hartley and Family
Illustrated by Al Hartley

A Barbour Book

The Teenage
Book of
Manners...
PLEASE!

Published by Barbour & Company, Inc.
    P.O. Box 719
    Uhrichsville, Ohio 44683
    http://www.barbourbooks.com

 Member of the
Evangelical Christian
Publishers Association

Printed in the United States of America.

CONTENTS

To the greatest teenagers
in the world — the teenagers
at Lilburn Alliance Church.

INTRODUCTION

It almost sounds like a contradiction in terms, or an oxymoron:

* like "jumbo shrimp"
* or "honest crook"
* or "holy war."

The two words "teenage" and "manners" just don't seem to go together.

Some folks feel that teenagers who enjoy belching contests, food fights and popping bubble gum wouldn't be caught dead with a manners book. True.

Today's teens don't want yesterday's etiquette book. They're more comfortable in jeans than a straight jacket.

So there's no nit-picking here. Just plain, practical tips on bringing out our best.

Read this user friendly book before graduation and go to the head of the class.

And do it with <u>class</u>.

Manners are to us what polish is to our cars— they make us <u>shine!</u>

We all enjoy adventure and the sense of discovery!

Well, come along ... Turn a few pages and discover exciting new things about life — and about yourself.

- Gain confidence.
- Feel better about yourself.
- Avoid embarrassing situations.
- Make friends easily.
- Become a leader.
- Be successful.

Big promises?

Sure!

But manners are like Domino's Pizza— guaranteed to deliver!

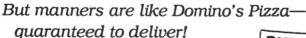

Manners not only open up a whole new world for us, they bury the old world of confusion and doubt.

For example:
What do we do with a
mouthful of lima beans that
is about to make us choke?

It's a problem but it's only temporary. One that goes much deeper is when we feel like a nerd, standing in a group with nothing to say. This one can shape our personality — maybe our future. That's why manners scratch us where we itch. They're more than a Band-Aid we put on and take off. They get down deep — to the heart of things. They develop our immune system against all the bruises and bumps of life. They put the fun back in.

HOW TO USE THIS BOOK

Each new chapter will introduce us to new manners. These manners are like new friends we want to get to know so we can feel comfortable with them.

We want to enjoy our new friends. They know all about acceptance, popularity and pollution-free living. And — get this — they know more about love than anyone else.

Manners are really a form of love. Simply a matter of giving the same kind of love we'd like to receive. Now, THAT can make life exciting!

"It [Love] is not rude."
1 Corinthians 13:5A

A Personal Comment
from the author

When I was in tenth grade, my mother gave me a manners books to read. At first I thought it was stupid and totally useless. But the more I read, the more I liked the idea. I suddenly realized, "Hey! The next time I'm on a date in a restaurant, I'll know exactly which fork to use, where to put my napkin, how to carry on a lively conversation and all sorts of other practical things."

Soon teachers at school, parents of my friends and others began to comment about my manners. It made me feel good about myself and it also seemed to put others around me at ease.

The book I read is now out of print ... even if it weren't it would need to be updated. Therefore, we've written this book as a family project ...

- I am doing the writing.

- My mother is the etiquette expert.

- My father is the cartoonist.

- My oldest son Fred and my daughter Andrea are the critics who make sure each new chapter makes sense.

Our objective is to make this book accurate, helpful, relevant and visual. It's fast moving, broken down into bite-sized pieces so you can get to know and make friends with one manner at a time.

Let's meet our first new friend.

Chapter 1

EFFECTIVE INTRODUCTIONS

The first manner we want to make friends with is *introductions,* for obvious reasons. Introductions allow us to make friends with everyone else.

We all know "First impressions are often lasting impressions" so we want to make a good start.

How would we rather be remembered?

Column A or column B?

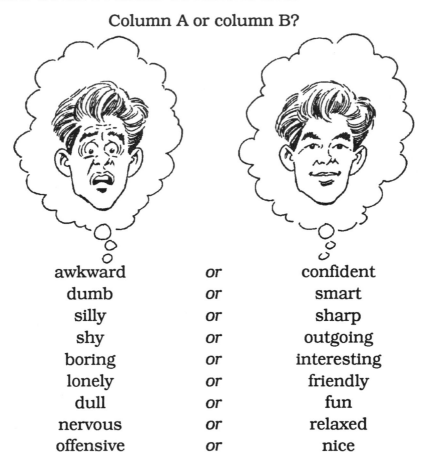

awkward	*or*	confident
dumb	*or*	smart
silly	*or*	sharp
shy	*or*	outgoing
boring	*or*	interesting
lonely	*or*	friendly
dull	*or*	fun
nervous	*or*	relaxed
offensive	*or*	nice

Actually, every introduction is sort of like Academy Awards Night and we're "on stage." We can either go home with egg on our face or win an Oscar.

Here's how to be a winner.

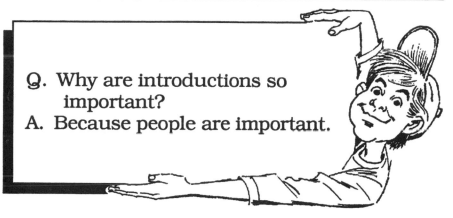

Q. Why are introductions so important?
A. Because people are important.

When we first meet a person, we want to immediately communicate to them that they're special. We're *truly* "glad to meet them."

Here are six basic guidelines to introductions:

1. Always stand.
2. Always smile.
3. Always look the person in the eye.
4. Always shake hands — firmly.
5. Always listen carefully.
6. Always greet them with their names.

(Read those guidelines again!)

Now let's take a closer look.

Obviously, all systems are on alert status. And why not? Every introduction is a new beginning—one of life's happy accidents perhaps.

We never know where a relationship will go, or what it might achieve. This can be high adventure!

We want to do *our* part.

1. **ALWAYS STAND.**

Standing immediately expresses, "You are important enough to me to get me out of my seat." On the other hand, if we simply remain seated when we greet someone, we are communicating something quite different: "You don't mean much to me; you're not worth the energy to get up." Manners teach us to stand in honor of people's significance. We certainly want to learn to treat people with respect.

Thought:

Our manners show others what we think of them. They also show others what they should think of us.

2. ALWAYS SMILE.

Much of our communication is nonverbal. A smile is the way our faces say, "It's nice to meet you." It's a way to put others at ease. We all know people who rarely smile. Such people seem to be self-centered, awkward, withdrawn or even angry. They make us feel uneasy and uncomfortable. Well, we don't want to make others feel uneasy around us. This is why a genuine smile is a good way to break the ice and express acceptance, favor and respect. Try it! You'll be amazed at the difference a simple smile makes.

Thought:
If someone doesn't have a smile, give them one of yours!

3. ALWAYS LOOK THE PERSON IN THE EYE.

"The eye is the window into the soul." Eye-to-eye contact is an expression of interest, attention and confidence. If we fail to look another in the eye it may indicate a disinterest or a lack of focus in the conversation, as if we are not interested enough to even look at the person. Failure to look eyeball to eyeball can also indicate an inner weakness or insecurity. If we notice our own inability to look people in the eye, we need to diagnose the cause and work to overcome it. Eye-to-eye contact is crucial for an effective introduction.

TRY IT, YOU'LL LIKE IT!

I gaze into her shining eyes.
With joy my soul transcends,
And yet, I wonder, is it love
Or shiny contact lens?
                                    Shelby Friedman

4. ALWAYS SHAKE HANDS—FIRMLY.

Every culture has a physical expression of greeting. Each is a form of respect and friendship.

Some
people
bow

others kiss on each cheek.

Our culture shakes hands. It's our way of making contact and breaking down initial social barriers.

When it comes to
shaking hands there
are two extremes:

• Some handshakes are limp as if
   grabbing a dead snake — *gross!*

• Others shake hands with the
   gusto of a nutcracker —
   ouch!

Avoid either extreme. Make your
handshake as friendly as your
manners.

5. ALWAYS LISTEN CAREFULLY.
(Get the name right!)

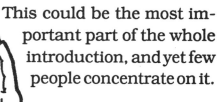

This could be the most important part of the whole introduction, and yet few people concentrate on it.

If you don't hear the name clearly, ask to have it repeated.

It won't reveal that you're a dork ... it'll show that you have respect for the one you're meeting and that you want to remember their name.

Thought:

Our name is one of our most important possessions.

6. ALWAYS GREET THEM WITH THEIR NAMES.

(Aren't we glad we listened carefully?)

"Good morning, Kathy. It's nice to see you."

Such a greeting should be loud and clear, just as solid as our handshake.

One of the most encouraging words for anyone to hear is the sound of his own name. Again, learning and using a person's name is another way of saying, "You're a significant person to me. You're worth enough for me to learn your name."

When We Don't Know a Name

In spite of our best efforts, sometimes names escape us. In such a case, we often feel like escaping, too, but there's a better way.

The direct approach:
"Hi, my name is Fred Hartley.
What's your name?"
The honest approach:
"Hi, I know we've met before, but I'm sorry,
I've forgotten your name. I'm Fred Hartley."

Maybe we know *them,* but we're not sure they know *us.* Be thoughtful.
"Hello, Mrs. Ledbottom, my name is Fred Hartley."

A Guideline:

Don't feel awkward. Remember
that considerate manners
always avoid embarrassment
and put others at ease.

"But when I meet new students, I don't know what to talk about with them. I hate it. I feel so awkward and out of place."

In the next chapter we'll look closer at some keys to meaningful conversation, but let's list several good questions that can help each of us develop effective communication skills.

"Where do you live?"
"How long have you lived here?"
"What school do you attend?"
"Are you involved with sports?"
"Do you have any brothers and sisters?"
"What do you enjoy doing after school or on weekends?"
"What music do you like to listen to?"

After you ask a question, listen to the response. It's quite natural and easy to comment on the answers you receive and to compare notes with your new friend. Before too long, you'll discover points of common interest that you can then discuss more fully.

How To Introduce People

Okay, we're comfortable meeting new friends. Now we'll look at how we introduce others.

In other words, it's Academy Awards Night and you're the M.C. Here's your cue card:

- Be sure the people you're introducing are paying attention to you.

- Repeat both names loud and clear.

- Try to put everyone at ease. *(It might help to mention something about them in addition to their names.)*
  "Justice Rehnquist is Chief Justice of the U.S. Supreme Court."

- When introducing an older person, use their name first.
  "Grandma, this is Sally. Sally, this is my grandma, Mrs. Smith."

- In large groups, only introduce your friend by name rather than everyone in the group.
  "Hey, everyone, this is Einstein. Would you please introduce yourselves to him."

- In a small group, introduce everyone by name."
  "Hey, everyone, this is Einstein, Einstein, this is Joe, Peter, Sam and Frankenstein."

Two Important Words
"Sir" and "Ma'am"

When speaking with adults, it is very polite to use the title "sir" when addressing men and "ma'am" when addressing women.

- "Grandma, I would like you to meet my friend Fred." I then reply with a smile, "It's very nice to meet you, *ma'am.*"

- Your friend's father asks you if you would like to eat pizza. "Yes, *sir*, pizza is one of my favorites!"

These two important words should be used when speaking with:
- a teacher
- a friend's parent
- any adult

**TRY THEM!
YOU'LL BE SURPRISED HOW MANY
MORE PIZZAS YOU'LL GET!**

JUST DO IT!

Tomorrow when you go to school or to church, immediately put these steps into practice with your teachers or other adults. They'll love it. Remember ...

- **Stand**
- **Smile**
- **Look** them in the eye
- **Listen** carefully
- **Shake** hands firmly
- **Use** their names

These are the six most basic steps of introductions and greetings. If we can master these six, we've already made a giant step toward our goal. Make friends with manners — they help us make friends with others.

Don't just read about manners; just do it!

BELIEVE ME, MANNERS AREN'T HEAVY!

A Personal Comment
— from the author

It's now up to you to make friends with effective introductions. It's not hard. Just begin to put these skills into practice.

It's just like making lay-ups or practicing cheers for cheerleading — the more you practice, the better you'll become.

Have fun!

Chapter 2

MEANINGFUL CONVERSATION

Once we have made *effective introductions*, we need to know how to carry on *meaningful conversations*.

┌─ INSIGHT ─────────────────────────────┐
We learn to talk when we are one or two years old,
but we learn to truly communicate
when we are teenagers.
└───────────────────────────────────────┘

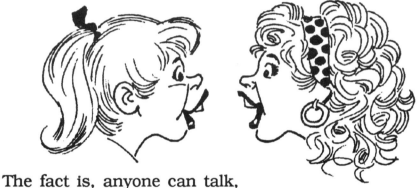

The fact is, anyone can talk,
but it requires skill to be able to communicate.

We all want to be able to participate intelligently in conversations, but only a few know how this is done.

An important part of learning the art of meaningful conversation is learning how to ask appropriate questions and to listen carefully to the answers.

Surface questions

- school, grades, activities
- hobbies, interests, music
- family, brothers, sisters

Meaningful questions

- **Goals**
  "What do you want to do when you graduate? College? Career?"
- **Thoughts**
  "What books have had the biggest influence on your life?"
- **Motives**
  "How do you want to be remembered by your friends at school?"
- **Purpose**
  "What is the most important thing in your life?"
  "Is there anything in your life you'd be willing to die for? What?"
- **Faith**
  "Do you know for certain that when you die you will go to heaven? Suppose for some unforeseen reason you were to die and stand before God, and he were to ask you, 'Why should I let you into my Heaven?' What would you say to Him?"

Obviously, deeper conversation takes time to develop, but as our friendship grows, so will our topics of conversation. Meaningful conversation is the key to developing meaningful and maturing friendships.

Asking good questions is important, but giving good answers is also important.

A good conversation is like playing catch with a baseball. If one person only catches the ball and never throws it back, before long both players will quit. In the same way, when we're asked a question, we need to respond with more than a simple yes or no, or worse yet, a feeble grunt. When asked a question, respond thoughtfully in some detail and then throw it back to the other person with something for them to interact with.

"Do you have any brothers or sisters?"

"Yes, I have one sister who is a cheerleader at Georgia Tech."

"Really? My dad graduated from Georgia Tech and we go to all the games."

"Wow! So do we. Aren't they the greatest?"

"Right! Will you introduce me to your sister?"

Use family mealtimes to talk about significant subjects. Try these key questions:

"What did you learn today that you never knew before?"
"Did anyone meet a new person today?"
"Hey, Dad, what do you think about ...?"
   Parents love to express their opinions. They also like feedback. Be sure to give them your impressions.
"Dad, do you like your job? Why? What's the most challenging part of it?"
"Mom, what do you admire about Dad?"
"Dad, what do you admire about Mom?"
"Did you face any disappointment today?"
"What do you hope to accomplish tomorrow?"

What does this have to do with manners?"

Meaningful communication is a key to manners. Why? Because it expresses genuine care. It says, "I care about what is happening in your life and in your brain." Good conversation is a skill we all need to work at developing.

GOOD LISTENING

Communication is a two-way street. Talking is only half the process. In fact, trying to develop a meaningful friendship simply by talking is like living at the end of a dead-end street.

Someone has said, "When God gave us two ears and only one tongue, it was His way of encouraging us to work twice as hard at listening as at talking."

Some simple secrets ...

Things to do

- Look the person in the eye to show attention.
- Smile to express interest.
- Nod your head to indicate that you understand what he is saying.

Things to avoid

- Don't yawn or fall asleep.
- Don't look at your watch or fidget.

These show disinterest.

CONVERSATION BUSTERS

Meaningful conversation leaves people feeling good about themselves.

But there are other conversations that are "off-limits."

> ### *It goes without saying ...*
> We should not participate in conversations that contain the following:
> - Private or confidential information
> - Dirty jokes
> - Ethnic jokes
> - Gossip: saying something about someone behind his back that we wouldn't say to his face
> - Flattery: saying something about someone to his face that we wouldn't say behind his back

If the conversation suddenly shifts to a topic that's off-limits we need to be free to say, "I don't want to talk about that any longer," or we want to simply start talking about something else. At times we might need to walk away.

> "Without wood a fire goes out;
> without gossip a quarrel dies down."
> *Proverbs 26:20*

MORE CONVERSATION BUSTERS

INSIGHT

There are certain areas of public conversation that are commonly understood as off-limits.

If we begin talking about these areas, it's like walking on thin ice. It makes us very vulnerable.

Before we know it, we may be in over our heads.

Topics commonly understood as off-limits ...

• **Money** — Questions about money usually come under the category of "none of your business."
   "How much did your house cost?"
   "How much does your dad earn a year?"
   "How much did you spend on your vacation?"

• **Sex** — Questions, jokes, or conversations about our private sexuality are always off-limits.
   "How far do you go on your date?"
   "Did you see Tom's new X-rated video?"

• **Physical flaws** — Teasing is usually a destructive form of humor — a student who is over-weight, has a face covered with pimples or has some physical defect is already painfully aware of this problem and does not need re-minding.

Self-centered talk

When we excel in a certain area we naturally feel good about it. It's easy to get the urge to share our pleasure with others and that's fine. However, when our pleasure turns into their *displeasure* we've crossed from good to bad manners. Manners, like love, do not boast.

bore is someone who keeps talking after everyone has stopped listening.

When we look in the
mirror — the image we see
is what we get. However,
we have control
over the image we
project to others.

We want to
remember the
purpose of manners:
to make others feel
just how important
they are to us,
and to avoid
unnecessary
attention to ourselves.

Let another praise you, and not your own
mouth; someone else, and not your own lips.
Proverbs 27:2

Sincere Compliments

> "Let your conversation be always full of grace, seasoned with salt, so that you may know how to answer everyone." *Colossians 4:6*

Giving thoughtful , sincere compliments is like putting a little salt or lots of ketchup on french fries ... it brings out the best! It adds flavor to our conversation.

Now, we're not talking flavor like in applesauce or bologna. We mean real, honest-to-goodness compliments that simply pay credit where credit is due.

The best place to test drive your new manners is right around the house! That's right — try them on the ones who are closest to you — your own family.

First really look at your parents through the eyes of love.
- Man, you do a good job providing for me. These new jogging shoes are awesome!
- There is no one I'd rather have as a parent than you.
- Thanks for spending time with me on my homework!
- Thanks for dinner, Mom, especially the pie!
- Dad, you're handsome, no wonder Mom married you.
- Mom, you're beautiful, inside and out.

For a first-hand demonstration of how fantastically manners work, you can even try a compliment on your brother or sister. Go ahead, try it ... it won't hurt.

- My new sweater looks great on you.
- You know, we don't always get along, but I want you to know I really do care about you.
- Wow! You play a great game of tennis.
- We're family, and it means a lot to be able to talk to you.
- Your new girlfriend is a knockout.
  What does she see in you? (Just kidding.)
- I'm glad we're brothers.

For friends:

- It's fun to be with you.
- I sure admire your convictions.
- You've got a great sense of humor.
- You really make an impression — even my dog likes you.
- I'm glad to have a friend like you.

For teachers:

- I appreciate all the work you put into this class.
- You challenge me to think creatively.
- You've really made me excited about learning.
- Math isn't my favorite subject, but you make it interesting.

SUMMARY

Meaningful conversations take a relationship beneath the surface and develop meaningful friendships. Such communication is clearly a two-way street, involving both speaking and listening.

- Be an attentive listener with eye-to-eye contact.
- Become skilled at asking appropriate questions.
- Respond with more than a "yes" or a "no."
- Convince other people you're sincerely interested in their lives.

JUST DO IT

The skill of developing meaningful conversation is one that will help us through life no matter what career we enter. The sooner we develop the skill, the more successful we will become at it.

Parents or family members are the best people on which to practice. Right now, pick three people with whom you can carry on meaningful conversations. Write down their names. Then check the box when each action-project is completed.

☐ Name: _____

☐ Name: _____

☐ Name: _____

Manners are contagious.
The more you spread them around,
the more they will come back
to you.

Chapter 3

TELEPHONE MANNERS

As we consider manners that relate to meaningful conversation, we quickly think of where much of that conversation takes place ... the telephone.

Most teens spend considerable time on the telephone. Many already have their own phones — the rest wish they did.

However, just because teens use the telephone frequently doesn't mean they know how to use it properly. In fact, using it frequently without knowing proper manners may cause a number of bad habits to develop.

The telephone makes conversation more complex:

- We obviously lack eye contact.
  - We are unable to nod in affirmation.
    - All body language is useless.
    - It's far easier to become distracted while talking on the phone.

The telephone can be used.
The telephone can also be abused.

Let's take it from the beginning ... As if the telephone were just invented and we are among the first to use one.

When The Phone Rings

1. Use the proper greeting:
   "Hello."
   "Good morning."
   "Good evening."
2. Speak clearly and confidently.
   (If you *mumble*, go back to the begin-
   ning of this book and start over again.)

Remember, our faces can't be seen over the phone. Our voices have to "smile" for us. Our tone of voice often says much more than our words.

3. If the call is for someone else, say, "Just a moment, please. May I ask who's calling?" Then call the person to the phone — but don't *shout!*

4. If the call is for someone not at home, ask if the caller would like to leave a message or have their call returned. (Manners are considerate.) If there's a message, be sure to write it down immediately and make certain that it's delivered.

Dad —
Pres. Bush would like you to call him as soon as possible. He called at 8:15 tonight.
P.S.
He sounds like a neat guy!

If we're home alone and don't know the person calling, it's wise to give limited information. Follow all the steps of number 4 (above). Use "we" or "us" instead of "I" or "me" since those words are less likely to signal that we're alone.

Grandparents

In our generation, most young people don't live near their grandparents. If we're going to get to know them and treat them with the honor and respect they de-serve, we need to learn how to talk effectively with them on the telephone. Remember, they have a special place in our lives and we have a very special place in theirs.

When we answer the telephone and learn it's one of our grandparents, rather than immediately passing the phone to our parents, it's a valuable opportu-nity for us to tell them about some of the events in our lives.

We've got all kinds of things to tell our grandparents:
- Our classes at school
- A project we're working on
- Our friends
- A new CD
- A concert we went to
- Our new tropical fish or pet cat
- An athletic event
- Our favorite TV show
- A book we're reading

Ask them about ...
- What they have been doing
- How they're feeling
- When you'll see them next
- What they have planned for the weekend

Again, all this conversation communicates honor and respect to some very special people who deserve every bit of it.

"Children's children [grandchildren] are a crown to the aged and parents are the pride of their children."
Proverbs 17:6

When We Make A Phone Call

As soon as we make a phone call, we need to realize we're actually entering someone else's home. We're interrupting their space, and we need to be very polite and respectful.

1. Before we call we need to think through:
   - Friend's full name
   - Parents' names in case an adult answers the phone

2. When a young person answers the phone, properly greet them:
   - "Hello, this is Fred. May I please speak with Michael?"
   - If an adult female voice answers, say, "Hello, this is Fred Hartley. Is this Mrs. Jordan?" "Yes, Mrs. Jordan, it's nice to speak with you too. May I please speak with your son Michael?"
   - If an adult male voice answers, say, "Hello, Mr. Jordan, how are you today? May I please speak with Michael?"

Welcome To Our High-Tech World

W e're in our element now, gang! Who knows more about electronics than teenagers, right? We have our finger on all the right buttons, but don't forget the new one in the program — the manners button.

Answering Machines:
Even though we're talking to a machine, our manners begin at the sound of the beep.
- Give name and time of call
- Identify the person we are calling
- Leave phone number
- Request a return phone call at their convenience.
  "Hi, this is Fred Hartley. I'm calling for Bob. It's Tuesday, 2:00 p.m. My phone number is _____. Please call me at your convenience. And have a nice rewind."

Fine Tuning Our Telephone Manners

- Don't talk to people in the room while you're on the phone with someone else without saying, "Please excuse me, Michael, I need to ask my dad a question." Then when you return to your telephone conversation say, "Sorry about that. I'm back."

- Don't eat, drink, chew gum or blow your nose while on the phone. There is nothing more sickening than to listen to someone else pre-digest his food over the telephone. Since your mouth is next to a microphone, the person listening on the phone can hear every bite and chew better than you can. (GROSS!)

- Don't type, wash dishes, vacuum or do any other noisy activity while on the telephone. All these activities can be heard by the other person, and they all communicate, "You don't have my undivided attention; I have more important things to do than simply listen to you." If someone calls when we're in the middle of a project, it's proper to let them know, and to ask permission, to return to the call: "Hey Sally, I'm sorry but I'm almost finished with the dishes. May I call you back in ten minutes?" Usually this is acceptable.

Sure, it's a barrel of laughs ...

... **B**ut it's really not good form to listen in on someone's phone conversation. We're breaking privacy and violating a trust when we do. We surely wouldn't want the tables turned, and that focuses our concept of manners in a practical way: We simply treat others the way we'd like them to treat us. The good ol' Golden Rule.

An even greater violation of privacy is to tape record a phone call without permission. Again, you might produce a best-selling record of deceit that can't be erased.

Please don't make prank phone calls. This is another invasion of people's privacy, similar to breaking into their homes.

- If we dial a wrong number, we shouldn't hang up before we apologize. Be humble. Identify our mistake and give the other person the courtesy of an apology. It may be helpful to compare phone numbers to make sure you don't dial the same incorrect phone number a second time:

  "I'm very sorry, but I need to be sure I don't make the same mistake again. Is this _____?"

  If the number is _____, then you obviously are dialing correctly but you have an incorrect phone number. Check the telephone directory.

  If the number is not _____, then you probably have the correct phone number, but you are dialing it incorrectly. Dial it again.

- Do not stay on the phone too long. Tying up the line is annoying to others who are attempting to call, and it may prohibit someone from receiving a very important call, or even an emergency call. Ordinary telephone conversations should not exceed fifteen to twenty minutes except on special occasions.

JUST DO IT

Unplug two telephones from the wall jack and practice with a brother, sister or parent.

- First, you pretend to call your grandparents and the other person will pretend to be your grandparents.
  (Great acting experience!)

- Then, the other person should pretend to call into your home to speak to your father when he is not home and you answer the phone. _(You may be headed for a career in show biz.)_

You might feel strange doing this role play but you will be amazed how much more confident you will be afterward. _(Check tomorrow's mail for TV offers!)_

Manners are not simply to read about. Manners are friends we need to get to know. The better we know them, the more comfortable we will feel. Just do it.

SUMMARY

- Recognize the telephone is not a toy to play with; it's a tool to be used constructively.
- Each time we dial the phone we're going into someone's home, and that needs to be done with care and politeness.
- When answering the phone, we're representing our family and we should do so with respect and courtesy, communicating that we're glad the people called. We want others to think highly of our family.
- Have a smile in our voices.
- Use proper names.
- Use courtesy words like "please" and "thank you."
- Speak clearly and confidently.
- Now that we know how to make phone calls, be sure we know how to end them!

Chapter 4

PERSONAL MANNERS

Let's get personal.
- Most manners deal with how we treat other people.
- Personal manners deal with how we treat ourselves.

Let's face it.
- We weren't copied on a Xerox machine.
- We weren't stamped out of a mold.
- We didn't come off an assembly line.
- We weren't punched out with a cookie cutter.

Each of us is handcrafted.
- We're custom made.
- We're one of a kind.
- We're each a designer original.

"For you created my inmost being;
you knit me together in my mother's womb.
I praise you because I am fearfully and
wonderfully made;
your works are wonderful,
I know that full well."
Psalm 139:13-14

A Personal Word
— from the author
There is nothing more embarrassing than to discover too late that we have a problem with *personal* manners. No one likes to be teased about ...

- **Dandruff**
- **Pimples**
- **Body odor**
- **Bad breath**
- **Wax in our ears**

Often people joke about the lack of personal manners, but it seems no one ever helps us discover exactly how we should properly care for ourselves. If we fail to learn these principles, we will quickly lose friends and suffer painful public embarrassment.

Here are some helpful guidelines.

Hygiene is a word we don't often hear except in toothpaste ads. However, it's VERY important!

Hygiene:
1. A system of principles that preserves health.   2. The application of such principles to our lives.

1. HAIRCARE

Hair comes in a variety of colors, textures and styles. While the basic color and texture are God-given, the style and the grooming of our hair is our responsibility.

• Style of hair is ordinarily a matter of personal preference.

• Grooming is also a matter of personal preference, but it needs to follow certain acceptable standards. Hair should be washed at least every other day and at times every day, depending on our level of activity and the oil in our scalps. If dandruff is a problem, there are several good shampoos that will offer immediate help. Ask your local pharmacist for his or her advice in selecting the best product. Ask your mother or father if they have ever noticed dandruff being a problem for you. They'll be honest.

Most teens are virtuosos on the comb.

But a comb is only the beginning. Then there's blow drying, brushing — care to try curling? — spraying and moussing. Whew!

If our hair is to be our crowning glory, we need a coronation every morning. And, talk about ladies in waiting, no one has yet calculated how many thousands across America wait outside the bathroom while the coronation is going on.

But hair takes care.

We all want to feel good about ourselves and the condition of our hair is important.

If you think haircare is a problem, ask the guy who doesn't have any!

2. BODY CARE

Body care is the opposite of body odor. There are several that must work together for us to maintain proper body care.

- *Bathing* — Usually it's a good habit to shower everyday. Showers don't need to last 20 minutes, but they should allow us to wash (or at least rinse) our hair and run the bar of soap over every part of our bodies. Be sure to rinse thoroughly! Ten minutes is plenty!

- *Proper soap* — Everyone has a different level of natural body oils. Soaps are rated accordingly: soap for oily skin, soap for normal skin, and soap for dry skin. You need to select the soap most appropriate for your skin.

DON'T FORGET THE IMPORTANCE OF EXERCISE!

• *Deodorant*—There are a variety of different styles, scents and ingredients in each deodorant. Styles include pump, aerosol spray, and roll-on. Scents and smells are grouped in two general areas, male and female. While deodorants are very personal, everyone should select a product and use it.

• *Cologne* — The purpose of the cologne is not to cover up a body odor that was not removed by proper bathing. It's purpose is to add a pleasant fragrance to a natural smelling body that has already been properly bathed.

SOME WARNINGS:
• Don't waste your cologne by bathing in it. This becomes overpowering and results in driving people away rather than attracting them.
• Don't waste all your money on super expensive brands. There are plenty of good fragrances that are reasonably priced.

3. TOOTH CARE

> Our hair can look great and our body can smell great, but if our teeth are covered with moss or our breath smells sour, we'll send some people running for cover.

Proper dental care is not the primary responsibility of a dentist or a dental hygienist. Proper dental care is the primary responsibility of every one of us. Yes, we should utilize the expertise of the professionals twice each year, but we should properly brush our teeth twice each day.

- *Brushing*—A good toothbrush and an effective toothpaste are the standard tools of proper dental care. These should be used at least twice a day, first thing in the morning and last thing in the evening. Ideally, brushing should be done following every meal to remove food particles from our teeth immediately.

- *Mouthwash* — When brushing after each meal is not possible, it is a good idea to utilize a pleasant and effective mouthwash. Swishing a single mouthful back and forth over our teeth will dislodge most unwanted food particles and will also give us delightful, fresh-smelling breath.

• *Flossing* — Dental floss is a most effective means of dislodging food particles and bacteria from between our teeth, where normal brushing can never reach. Floss is available in pleasant-tasting flavors and it should be used every evening prior to the final brushing of the day. Doing this removes the harmful bacteria and food particles that cause tooth decay while you sleep.

TOOTH TIPS:
• In addition to these primary tooth-care disciplines, it may be necessary to utilize a breath mint, mint chewing gum or mouth freshener to remove stubborn bad breath.
• Your mother or father are usually the best to ask, "Do I have bad breath?" Be true to your teeth or they'll be false to you. *(Sure, it's an oldie but it's a goodie.)*

4. FACE CARE

The teenage years bring with them a wide variety of physical changes during what is known as puberty.

Many of these changes affect our complexion. Hormones within the body cause our skin to produce oil. When pockets of oil become trapped underneath the skin, they become infected and develop into *pimples* (also called acne). There are some simple, easy steps we can take to minimize our skin problems.

> *Puberty*: The normal state of physical development within both boys and girls when sexual reproduction first becomes possible. For boys this usually takes place at 14 years old. For girls this usually takes place at 12 years old.

- Wash our faces with soap and a washcloth three times a day.
- Wash our hair everyday and keep it off our foreheads.
- Do not touch our faces with our hands. Oil and dirt will wipe off on our faces and cause problems.

If acne becomes a more severe problem, we should consult our family doctor who will recommend a change in our diets, additional skin cleanser and possible medication. The first foods to avoid include chocolate and peanut butter.

FOR BOYS ONLY:

Sooner or later, proper face care will involve shaving, and the motto is, "better sooner than later." Once the original facial hair known as "peach fuzz" starts growing, we need to shave at least twice a week. As soon as the baby hair begins forming into coarser hairs, we need to shave everyday. Usually these coarser hairs grow first around the ears as sideburns or on our upper lips.

There are two types of razors:

1. The manual blade, used with shaving cream. Such a razor blade gives a good, clean shave, but it does risk a nick which might draw a little blood. A successful shaving technique is usually easy to develop. Follow the principle "Easy does it." When you start, take your time and press lightly.
2. The electric razor. These are more expensive, but they work effectively and usually do not risk a facial nick.

Whichever system of shaving you choose, don't wait too long until you start using it consistently.

FOR GIRLS ONLY:

Women don't spend considerable time removing facial hair but they have a wide variety of products to choose from that provide proper facial care.

- **Lipstick**
- **Eyeshadow**
- **Eyeliner**
- **Mascara**
- **Blush**
- **Eyelash curler**

While using each of these products is fun and exciting, the chronic danger is overkill. We need to remember ...
- True beauty does not come out of a bottle.
- Make-up should never draw attention to itself. It should only accent the natural beauty of the person wearing it.

Young women will learn to shave legs and underarms. *(The same tips given to boys on the previous page apply here.)*

5. NAIL CARE

Our hands are an important part of our bodies. They reflect our personalities. We need to care for them properly by keeping them clean and neat.

Nails need to be kept clean. Each of us needs his own nail clippers that we should use once a week to clip and clean both our fingernails and toenails.

Boys keep their fingernails clipped short.

Girls allow approximately a quarter-inch length to be maintained symmetrically. If used, nail polish should be maintained every week.

NOTICE:
Nail biting is forbidden!
If you are in the habit,
quit today
or
it's back
to
Chapter 1 again!

6. PROPER POSTURE

Often without realizing it, we project an image of ourselves by the way we stand.

PUZZLE PICTURE:
FIND THE
COUCH POTATO.

not confident	or	confident
sad	or	happy
depressed	or	optimistic
lonely	or	friendly

Unless we have a physical defect, posture is controllable.

- Drooping shoulders
- Lazy arms
- Sad expressions

... are all things we can control.

It might take a little effort, but it is worth it. Stand up straight, walk tall, step with confidence.

7. PROPER FOOD AND DRINK

Putting good, healthy food in our stomachs is like putting good clean gas in an automobile. If, on the other hand, we put junk food into our stomachs, it is like putting sludge into the gas tank of an automobile. We will get fat and sluggish and we will not be able to think as clearly.

JUNK FOODS
candy bars
doughnuts
french fries (with ketchup)
sodas
ice cream
deep-fried chicken
cake
white breads
greasy hamburgers

HEALTHY FOODS
fresh fruit
salads
vegetables
pizza
low-fat milk
ice water
fruit juices
cheese
dried fruits
whole-grain breads
nuts

8.   PROPER SLEEP

As we give care to our bodies, we need to understand
that our bodies require proper sleep. Without proper
sleep, we can become irritated and our bodies are
more susceptible to sickness.

Most people require six to eight hours of sleep each

night. Healthy, growing teenagers can require eight to ten
hours of sleep each night. When strenuous physical exercise is added to a daily activity, you might need to add an
extra hour of sleep.

INSIGHT:

"For he [God] grants sleep to those he loves."
Psalm 127:2b

9. **PROPER DRESS**

Obviously, it is impossible to adequately cover this enormous subject within a manners book. Most clothing choices are a matter of personal preference. However, we all need to understand the two basic categories of dress up and dress down.

- **Dress up**

There are times when we will be expected to dress up. For boys, this usually requires a shirt, tie, dress pants, sports jacket, socks and leather shoes *(not sneakers!)*. For girls, it requires at least a skirt or dress, panty hose and dress shoes.

Occasions normally requiring such dress include:

- Church or synagogue
- Graduations
- Special family gatherings: Christmas, Thanksgiving, Easter
- Weddings
- Fancy restaurants

> **Formal wear:** The most formal attire is a tuxedo for men and a formal or full-length gown for women. This is usually only worn at a prom or grad night, or at a wedding.

• Dress down

After a more formal event is over, we are free to change into more casual clothes. This is called "dressing down." There is a wide range of casual dress that is acceptable depending on the occasion.

Nice Casual Clothes

For boys — dress shirt with short or long sleeves, dress pants, socks and leather shoes.
For girls — skirt with matching blouse.

Casual Clothes

For boys — cotton or knit collared shirt, pants or jeans, and shoes.
For girls — pants or dress shorts, skirt, most shoes.

Work / Play Clothes

For boys — T-shirt, shorts, sweatsuit, sneakers.
For girls — same.

While we each show our own personality and individuality by the way we dress, we need to understand these basic guidelines. If we fail to understand, we might end up with something that looks pretty silly.

PEOPLE ARE LESS LIKELY TO NOTICE YOUR CLOTHES,
IF YOU WEAR A BIG SMILE!

SUMMARY

Good manners involve good personal hygiene. Clean, healthy people are more likely to develop wholesome friendships.

Caring properly for our bodies is not selfish, it's smart and sociable. In a sense it's our duty.
1. We owe it to our friends to be presentable.
2. We owe it to ourselves to treat our bodies with respect.
3. We owe it to God who designed us.

> "Do you not know that your body
> is a temple of the Holy Spirit,
> who is in you,
> whom you have received from God?
> You are not your own; you are bought
> at a price.
> Therefore honor God with your body."
> *1 Corinthians 6:19-20*

ARE YOU WEARING GOD'S LABEL?

Chapter 5

PERSONAL VALUES

Personal *manners* keep us clean on the *outside*. Personal *values* keep us clean on the *inside*.

If the *outside* isn't right, our behavior, our breath and our body odor will turn people off. We could throw a party in a phone booth for our friends.

If the *inside* isn't right (our values), all the mouth wash, spray cans and fancy etiquette in the world won't cover up the percolating self-destruction about to happen.

We could be the most popular teen in town, but, without values, our friends would be the kind that make sensational statistics, not healthy, positive relationships.

Something of Value

Girls with *glamour* impress guys by the way they *look!*

Girls with *values* impress guys by the way they *are!*

Values make a big difference in our lives. They're like deadbolts on our homes — they keep us from being broken into and ripped off.

There are many personal values.

Let's look at just five.

1. The **value of truth.**
2. The **value of family.**
3. The **value of friends.**
4. The **value of sexuality.**
5. The **value of private property.**

Let's take a closer look and see what these values are worth to us.

1. The Value of Truth

> **Honesty is not just the best policy — it's the only policy!**

In a sense there's no higher value than the truth. All other values rise out of this one.

- If we're not truthful, we'll never have any true friends because no one will ever truly know us ... at least they'll never know who we really are.
- Oh, we might seem to impress people but they're not really impressed with us. They're impressed with the false image we project.
- Actually, if we're not truthful, we'll never grow up. Growing up means we're willing to be responsible for who we really are — not who we pretend to be.

> "You shall not give false testimony against your neighbor."
> *Exodus 20:16*

A Personal Word

—*from the Author*

If we've gotten into the habit of telling lies ... even little white lies ... now is the time to stop.

Lies are like snowballs: They keep getting bigger and bigger. If we start telling lies, we become fearful because soon we forget to whom we lied. We might even forget the truth ourselves. Such a web of lies will surely bug us and eventually trap us! When we stretch the truth, watch out for the snap back!

In order to break the habit, make an agreement with yourself right now that from now on you'll only tell the truth. If you should ever exaggerate or tell a baldfaced lie, you will immediately go to the person, correct the story and tell them the truth.

A number of years ago I made that agreement and it has come in handy many times. As far as I know, I've kicked the nasty habit of lying.

2. The Value of Family

It's easy for family members to take each other for granted. We want to do all we can to keep our family circle unbroken and blossoming.

A rose only becomes beautiful and blesses others when it opens up and blooms.

We want to bloom where we're planted:
• Spend special time talking to each parent and each brother and sister.
• Do acts of friendship (washing dishes, mowing lawn, keeping room clean, etc.).
• Want to see other family members succeed.
• Take vacation time with the family.
• Pray for each family member by name.
• Frequently use the magic words "please" and "thank you."
• Keep complaining to a minimum.
• Give hugs and kisses and laughs.

Children, obey your parents in the Lord, for this is right. "Honor your father and mother" —which is the first commandment with a promise— "that it may go well with you and that you may enjoy long life on the earth."   *Ephesians 6:1-3*

3. The Value of Friends

A true friend is a real treasure. We're not talking about someone who happens to ride on the school bus with us. We mean someone we're really close to.

If we have a good friend, we don't need a mirror. In other words, a real friend is honest and dependable. We can talk over things in confidence with them. We can share our deepest feelings and be sure that it's "just between the two of us."

On the other hand, sharing something with the aquaintance on the school bus might be like having a microphone in our hand and shouting,

"ATTENTION ALL K-MART SHOPPERS."

We know the news will spread all over the mall.

True friends, like our mirrors, always tell us the truth rather than what they think we'd like to hear.

"A friend loves at all times, and a brother is born for adversity."
Proverbs 17:17

It's helpful to understand that there are different levels of friendships. As our friendships mature, they'll become more and more meaningful.

Acquaintances:
(Most of those on the school bus)

We know their names but we know very few other details of their lives.

Surface Friends:
(Many of our classmates)

We go to the same school or church, or live in the same neighborhood, or play on the same athletic teams. We have similar interests but we don't necessarily share the same values.

True Friends:
(Numbering as many as the fingers on our hands)

We might share common interests. We do share similar values. We actively and creatively help each other reach common goals.

Intimate Friends:
(The fingers on one hand)

We have the same life goals. We're challenging each other with projects to develop God-given potential.

4. The Value of Our Sexuality

Our own sexuality is a very special gift. It's so special that it needs to be held in honor, and protected.

Our sexuality is private.

Sex is not a dirty word; it's a holy word and it needs to be treated with great respect.

> A generation that values human sexuality will hold strict moral standards.

> • We should set strong moral standards that we refuse to compromise even if it means losing dates.
>
> *"Associate with friends of good quality if you esteem your own reputation. It's better to be alone than in bad company."*
>
> George Washington

• We should determine ahead of time that we will save ourselves sexually until we are married.

• We avoid careless talk about sex or joking about it. Locker-room humor is off limits.

• If we're at a movie or at a friend's house watching a movie that's immoral, we'll walk out or change the channel.

• We will not defile ourselves physically or mentally.

> **VIRGIN:** *One who is pure and modest. One who has not had sexual intercourse.*

5. The Value of Private Property

When we demonstrate the value of private property, we show proper respect for our possessions and the possessions of others.

- We'll take good care of all our possessions.
    — our clothes, shoes, etc.
    — our tapes and CD's   — our car
    — our toys   — the family TV

- We'll understand and respect the value of a dollar.
— we'll not waste our money.

- We'll keep our room neat.

- We'll not steal the property of others.
- When we borrow anything we'll return it in as good or better shape than when we borrowed it.

A generation that values private property prosecutes thieves.

A Personal Word ...

From the Author

Learning the value of private property involves learning the value of the dollar.

Most students feel as though they never have enough money. However, according to the Associated Press, America's 29 million teenagers spend $65 billion a year ... or $2,200 each.

An estimated $35 billion is Mom and Dad's money.

An estimated $30 million is from teenagers' pockets.

No matter which way you look at it, this is a lot of money. Items most frequently purchased include ...

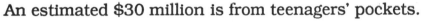

- fast foods
- soft drinks
- shampoo
- deodorant
- clothes
- gas, car
- ice cream
- gum
- movie tickets
- video tape rentals
- CD's or cassettes

While we'd all enjoy having more money, it's important for us to learn to appreciate and properly invest the money we already have. In addition to buying items for our own use, we want to learn to ...

- save some for college, a car or other future goals.
- save some for Christmas, birthday, and anniversary gifts for our family members.
- give a portion to worthy causes such as your local church or an underprivileged family.

Chapter 6

TABLE MANNERS

Mealtime is a time of enrichment and fulfillment. No pun intended. We can't wait to see what Mom brings to the table and, in a sense, the most important thing on the menu is the kind of manners that we bring to the table. A dinner fit for a king would quickly lose its flavor if we were eating with a slob or someone who disliked table talk.

For example, who would you rather eat with?

- One who chews with mouth open
- One who slurps his soup
- One who spits food back on plate (gross!)

- One who chews with mouth closed
- One who drinks soups from spoon
- One who discreetly removes food from mouth.

Okay, dinner's ready! Let's eat together!

FIRST, OUR TOOLS

Forks, knives and spoons are called utensils. We all need to learn both how to set a table and how to properly use each utensil.

COMMON PLACE SETTING

When our parents ask us to "set the table," this arrangement is the common place setting.

FORMAL PLACE SETTING

At formal banquets or fancy restaurants, you will sit at tables with many more utensils than we are normally familiar with.

SEQUENCE

There's a very easy way to remember which utensils to use first. Essentially you work from the outside to the inside; from the utensils farthest from the plate, moving in toward the plate.

For example . . .
1. As soon as you sit down, the napkin is placed on your lap.
2. Once your food is served you will use your "fish fork" to eat the hors d'oeuvres and/or your soup spoon to drink your soup - quietly!
3. Your salad will then be served and you will often use your teaspoon to stir your beverage.
4. When dinner is served you will use your dinner fork and knife.
5. With the meal you will also use your butter knife and plate for the bread.
6. Finally, after the meal you will use either your dessert fork or spoon, depending on what is served.

USING THE PROPER GRIP

Just as there is a proper way to grip a tennis racket or golf club, so there is a proper way to hold a spoon, fork or knife.

For normal use, a spoon, fork or knife should be held similar to the way we hold a pen or pencil, only closer to the other end.

When cutting food, we use a different grip.

- Use short cuts to avoid rocking the entire table back and forth.
- Avoid unnecessary sounds while cutting — clanging silverware to plate, or screeching utensils together.
- Cut one piece of meat at a time, or at the most two pieces. Eat them before cutting any more.
- Place knife on plate between mouthfuls. You never hold the knife in one hand while feeding yourself with the fork from the other hand (unless you are European, in which case this is acceptable).
- Cut all pieces small enough so they can be placed comfortably in your mouth — no matter how hungry you are.

WARNING: DO NOT COPY THIS ILLUSTRATION.

The only utensils used to put food in your mouth are the fork and spoon — never the knife. The spoon *is only* used for soup and dessert, not for drinking coffee or for eating the meal.

While you are still eating, keep your knife and fork on your plate. Do not place them back on the table after using them, or partly on your plate and partly on the table.

When you have finished your meal, place your knife and fork on your plate parallel to each other. This will indicate to your waiter/waitress that you have completed your meal.

QUICK QUIZ: We've finished our meal. Are the untensils below sending the right signal to the service person?
NO! The plate above is correct.

THE NAPKIN

The napkin is one of our best friends at the dinner table. As we've already discovered about other manners, the napkin is designed to keep us from public embarrassment and needs to be kept within reach at all times.

- As we approach a dinner table we will notice the napkin is usually folded to the left of the place setting. Occasionally it will be folded on the dinner plate or perhaps even inserted in the drinking glass to the right of your plate.

- As soon as we sit down, we need to place the napkin on our laps. This needs to become a conditioned response — something we do automatically.

- Using the napkin at meals also needs to be done properly. It is not a bib to be tucked in our shirt collars or tied around our necks. It is not a handkerchief. Never use it to blow your nose — never! It is not a towel with which to wipe your whole face.

It must only be used to blot our mouths. We normally only need to use a single corner of the napkin through the entire meal. We should become skilled enough to navigate the spoon and fork into our mouths without leaving considerable food on our faces. If we dirty our napkin too severely, it can hardly be placed back on our laps without staining our clothes.

A napkin should not be wadded up into a little ball. It should be left extended so that it can always lie flat on our laps.

THE BEVERAGE

There are essentially three basic shapes from which we drink.

The normal glass:

This is to be held toward the bottom of the glass so fingers never touch the place our lips touch while drinking. All glasses are to be placed away from the table to avoid unnecessary spills.

The goblet:

This is to be held by the bottom of the bowl, not by the stem, or by the base. Holding the bowl allows us to get a better grip.

The cup:

This is to be held by the handle. If the cup contains a hot beverage, it is almost impossible to hold the cup itself. The handle is designed to avoid burning. Use it.

Eating, like drinking, is to be done as quietly as possible. No slurping. No sloshing. No burping. Please!

SITTING AT THE TABLE

When eating at our homes, we usually have the same seat at each meal. When eating at a friend's house, we wait until the host or hostess indicates where we should be seated. At more formal banquets, there will even be place cards indicating where we shall sit.

- We should not sit down until the hostess is seated or until she asks us to sit.
  - Men should pull out the chairs for the women next to them, helping them to be seated first.

BASIC GUIDELINES FOR SEATING

- Hostess is seated first. Women sit before men. Sit up straight. Do not rock the back two legs of your chair.
- Keep your feet to yourself — no kicking!
- Keep your elbows to yourself — no jabbing, especially when cutting your food.
- Keep your napkin flat on your lap.
- Enjoy good, creative conversation, as well as good food.

SOUP

Soup is spooned away from us. (There are many theories about why this rule was started, but most agree it is a weird rule. The problem is, if we do not follow it, we will be weird!)

Never blow soup and never slurp. If it is too hot, we should skim the top of the bowl with our spoons.

When using a larger soup spoon, we never stick the entire spoon in our mouths. We drink from the tip or side.

Nearing the bottom of the bowl, we may tilt the bowl to get the last bit of soup, still spooning away from us. When finished, we leave the spoon in the bowl or on the plate beneath the cup. Never put the spoon back on the table.

THE BLESSING

Since meal-times are special times, before we eat it's a good idea to say a short and simple prayer of thanksgiving to God. This is called grace, the blessing, or returning thanks.

It is the responsibility of the host or hostess to decide whether or not to say the blessing. If we're in the habit of thanking God for our food prior to eating every meal and our host does not take the initiative, it is not polite to say anything about it. Simply thank God silently for your food and then enjoy the meal.

On the other hand, if you are the host and you have friends to your house or to a restaurant, you should always feel free to lead in a short prayer. Simply say, "I always thank God for my food before I eat. Let me lead us." Then bow your head and pray:

> *"Father, thank you for providing this good food. I thank you for these good friends. Bless us as we enjoy this good time together. In Jesus' name. Amen."*

" ... foods, which God created to be received with thanksgiving... For everything God created is good, and nothing is to be rejected if it is received with thanksgiving, because it is consecrated by the word of God and prayer." *1 Timothy 4:3b-5*

WHEN MAY WE START EATING?

When all the runners are in place, it is the sound of a gun that begins a race. When everyone is seated, the hostess raises her fork from the table. That gesture indicates that the meal may begin.

If we have any doubts about the proper utensil to use, we keep our eyes on the hostess. She gives us more than the starting signal. Just use the same utensil she's using and we can't go wrong.

BREAD AND BUTTER

Bread and rolls, butter and jelly are to be placed on the bread and butter plate. We should not place butter directly from the butter plate to our bread.

We should break off a portion of the bread or roll, butter it and then eat it. Never butter the entire piece of bread or roll at one time.

We should take the piece of bread or the roll we touch. We should not pick up a roll and then put it back in preference of another.

PASSING FOOD

When passing a glass or cup, never touch the rim.

When passing serving dishes, always be sure to pass the serving spoon or fork with the dish. Never leave it on your own plate.

Food is normally passed to your right, counter-clockwise, unless your hostess directs differently.

Take only as much food as you can eat. When you serve yourself, be sure there is enough food to allow each person at the table a similar size serving. If we take some food we do not enjoy, we just leave it on our plates without commenting on our displeasure. *(We can think "yuk" but we can't say "yuk!")*

MISCELLANEOUS TABLE MANNERS

- Fried chicken should be eaten with knife and fork unless the hostess gives permission otherwise. On a picnic, fingers are fine.
- Always chew with our mouths closed. No one else wants to see or hear us eating.
- Never talk with a full mouth.
- Elbows are not to be rested on the table during the meal. Before and after the meal, it does not matter.
- Sit up straight. We should lift our food to our mouths. Never lower your head down to pick up our food.
- Normally you should only hold a single utensil at a time. The exception is when cutting food or when pushing small food (like peas) on to your fork. Then place the knife on your plate while you feed yourself.

If a certain food doesn't appeal to us, we graciously take a small amount. If eating it would call out the rescue squad, simply pass it by without comment.

• If we need to use the restroom we simply ask, "May I please be excused for a moment?" Do not ask, "May I please use your bath-room?"

• Never feed pets during dinner time. A bad habit.

• If we spill, we apologize and immediately offer to clean it up. It was obviously a mistake and should not ruin our meal.

• When squeezing a lemon, we cup our hand around it to avoid squirting across the room.

• At a formal ban-quet, whenever a woman rises from the table all men should also stand. The man seated nearest to her should help move her chair for her. When she re-turns, once again all men stand and reseat themselves only after she is seated.

DESSERT

For many of us, this is our favorite part of the meal. We certainly don't want to make any serious mistakes now.

• Spoons are used for soft desserts—custard, pudding, ice cream, sherbet.

• Forks are used for solid dessert—cakes, pies, most fruit.

• If nuts or candy are served, take a few and place them on your plate. Eat them from your own plate. Never eat them directly from the serving dish.

Even though we're into dessert, we want our manners to be still showing. If we'd like something on the table we ask to have it passed.

WE DON'T REACH!

GOOD CONVERSATION

While we have already talked about meaningful conversation in Chapter 2, *now* is the time to apply what we have learned. No matter how good the food may be, it always tastes better with good conversation.

• Try to have some conversation with everyone at the table.

• If anyone at the table is sitting silently, ask creative questions to draw them into discussion.

• If you have recently seen a movie or read a book, only share important details or general observations. No one enjoys a total recap.

• Dinner conversation should be positive and pleasant, nothing too heavy. No arguments — they tend to cause indigestion.

• When talking at the table, do not speak with your hands — certainly not while holding utensils.

AFTER THE MEAL

- While we thank God before the meal, it is always nice to thank the hostess or the cook after the meal.

- Before we rise from our places, we should always ask the hostess, "May I please be excused?"
- At our own home we always want to clear our plate and glass. When visiting in a friend's home, we should offer to help.
- When we rise from the table, we should push our chairs back under the table. Our napkins should be placed unfolded next to our plates.

FOOD FOR THOUGHT

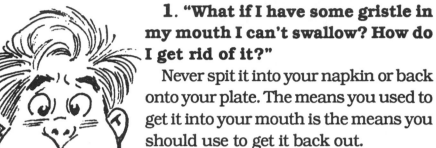

1. **"What if I have some gristle in my mouth I can't swallow? How do I get rid of it?"**

Never spit it into your napkin or back onto your plate. The means you used to get it into your mouth is the means you should use to get it back out.

• If it is gristle from meat, you put it into your mouth by fork, so remove it from your mouth by fork.

• If it is a bad clam from your soup which you ate by spoon, remove it by spoon.

• If it is the pit from your olive which you ate by hand, remove by fingers.

2. **"May I blot up my gravy with bread or a roll?"**

Yes! Just do it with your fork, using smaller mouth-sized pieces of bread. Using your fingers might be messy!

3. **"May I use a knife as a 'pusher' when eating peas or corn?"**

Yes! You may also use you roll as a pusher. Just do not eat with both hands. After you have used your fork to eat your corn, put down your fork and then take a bite of roll.

4. "What if I spill?"

Hey, we all spill. We all make mistakes when we eat. Obviously we try to eat as mannerly as possible but when we spill, we apologize, help clean it up, and enjoy the rest of the meal.

5. "What if I just have to burp?"

There is an old saying,

> *"'Tis better to burp and bear the shame, than to squelch the belch and bear the pain."*

Believe it or not, while belching is not preferable, it is not intolerable. However, it should be done quietly and as infrequently as possible. (Some teenagers seem to burp through a megaphone and with great repetitiveness. This **is** intolerable.) If you must burp, do it once and say, "Excuse me" to no one in particular. If you must burp a second time, excuse yourself from the table.

6. **"What if I get food caught between my teeth?"**

If your tongue is unable to remove the food (with your mouth closed, of course) wait until after the meal and find a toothpick or use dental floss in the privacy of your own bathroom. Toothpicks are unacceptable at the dinner table.

7. "What if the person next to me is making me sick because of all the noise he is making eating with his mouth open?"

Do not correct the person during the meal. This is usually too embarrassing even among friends. However, if you care about the person, do them a favor — tell him his problem after the meal is over in private.

You may even want to give him a copy of this book!

8. "What if I'm at a friend's house and I don't like any of the food served?"

Take a very small portion of the least repulsive food served. There must be something you can eat without getting sick. Be sure to compliment your host on the effort he or she put forth in preparing the meal, even if you can't sincerely compliment the meal itself.

SUMMARY

BEFORE MEALS:
- Use restroom
- Wash hands
- Wait for hostess to be seated
- Place napkin on lap
- Thank God
- Wait for hostess to raise her fork

DURING MEALS:
- Chew with mouth closed
- Pass food to the right
- Use "please" and "thank you"
- Practice good posture
- Enjoy good conversation

AFTER MEALS:
- Ask to be excused
- Thank hostess/cook for the meal
- Clear your plate, utensils and glass
- Push your chair under the table

JUST DO IT

Manners are not usually learned all at once. It takes time.

"If I had to think about all these rules, I wouldn't enjoy my food."

Rather than trying to implement all these guidelines, read back through the chapter and select three manners you would like to begin practicing now. When you have made your selections, write them down in the spaces below.

1. _____

2. _____

3. _____

Chapter 7

RESTAURANT MANNERS

We all enjoy eating out. And we all have our favorite restaurants.

There's a whole smorgasbord of restaurants to choose from, but basic manners apply to each style. However, it's helpful to understand the differences in eating places.

FAST FOOD

By far, the most common and often the most fun are fast-food restaurants. It's not even necessary to get out of the car. Just roll down the window and speak into the microphone.

- We usually order our food at the counter and then carry our food to the table on a tray or in a bag.
- While we don't use silverware and we don't have a formal place setting, it's still a good idea to ...
  — Be sure everyone in your "party" has his food before you start eating. (Considerate)
  — Place the food properly on the table with all necessary napkins and condiments. (Careful)
  — Remove trays. (Practical)
  — Thank God for the food. (Grateful)
  — Begin eating together (unless we're with the entire senior class).
  — Don't forget to clean up as you leave. (Harmony)

CAFETERIA

A cafeteria is similar to most school lunch lines (pardon the expression!). Plates, utensils and napkins are alongside the trays at the beginning of the serving line.

**RED ALERT!
RED ALERT!**
As we pass along the food line and make our selection, it's very easy to "pig out." So many of the foods seem to wink at us and say "Please pick me up." Actually, a buffet line is a fantastic training ground for life. We learn, one way or another, that we just can't have everything.

- Most cafeterias have people to collect trays. If not, we simply place our trays on the nearby tray stand.
- Most cafeterias also provide people to clean tables. If no one is available to do this, we want to take care of it ourselves out of consideration.

FAMILY RESTAURANTS

- Family restaurants offer sit-down dinners. That is, we don't stand in line for our food as we do for fast-food or in a cafeteria. The food is brought to us. Family restaurants have a much larger selection of food than fast-food restaurants and are more affordable than a gourmet restaurant.
- When we're shown to our table, we'll usually find our silverware wrapped in our napkin. In such a case, it's our job to set the silverware out as we would when eating at home.
- Family restaurants do not always provide butter plates. Therefore, we put our butter and bread on our dinner plates, never on the bare table.
- As we use cracker papers or butter wrappings, we place the empty material in the ashtray or under our plates.

> *Never feel embarrassed to bow your head*
> *in a restaurant and thank God for your food.*

"FANCY" GOURMET RESTAURANTS

Each of us will have opportunity to
eat at a fancy restaurant perhaps
at:
• parents' anniversary.
• a wedding.
• prom or graduation banquet.
• other special occasions.
• We'll want to dress for the occasion: tie and jacket for the young
  men, and a dress for the young
  women. At such times it may be appropriate for the man
  to purchase a corsage for the woman.
• The man who shows us to the table is the *maitre 'd.*
  Since the meal *is gourmet,* it will be more expensive.
  Therefore, it's thoughtful not to order a meal that's more
  expensive than the person paying the bill can afford. If
  we're paying, the
  choice is ours.
• If we drop silver-
  ware, leave it on
  the floor. It's
  neither sanitary
  nor mannerly to
  pick up dropped

> *Gourmet:* Someone who is an
> excellent judge of fine food
> and drink.

utensils. Your waiter will be glad to replace it. Please!

THE MENU

There are two basic types of food service in a restaurant:
- *Table d'hote*: one price for a complete meal.
- *À la carte*: each course is priced separately.

We should read our menu carefully or inquire before ordering, if we're in doubt. A full meal includes an appetizer, soup, salad, main course (entrée), dessert, and beverage. If we know we can't eat that much, we can ask to skip one or two courses, or we may order à la carte. Many restaurants include a salad and a vegetable with our entrée. Feel free to inquire.

Many finer restaurants offer a small sorbet (sherbet) after the salad course. This chills the taste buds and clears the salad flavor for the main course, but it usually comes as a surprise to most diners (a happy one, for children).

Crackers are served with the soup course. No matter what we do at home, this is not the time to crumple up the crackers and drown them in our soup.

Menus may contain foreign words that we don't comprendez. Our service person will be glad to explain any words or dishes that raise questions.

FOREIGN WORDS ON MENUS

à la	in the style of
à la king	in cream sauce
almandine	with almonds
au jus	in its own juice
bon bon	candy
crêpe	thin pancake
croutons	diced toasted bread
demitasse	strong black coffee
en croute	baked in pastry crust
escargot	snails
filet mignon	grilled choice beef
flambée	served flaming
florentine	with spinach
frappé	chilled
fruits de mer	seafood
garni	decorated
gratiné	topped with bread crumbs and cheese
hors d'oeuvres	appetizers
julienne	thin strips
lait	milk
légumes	vegetables
madrilene	clear chilled soup
maison	house (restaurant)

MORE FOREIGN WORDS ON MENUS

mornay	white cheese sauce
mousse	light dessert of cream and eggs
omelette	egg dish
parfait	iced dessert
petit	small
poisson	fish
purée	mashed
quiche	a tart of eggs and cheese
sorbet	fruit sherbet
soufflé	puffed dish with eggs, cheese, etc.
tart	small fruit pie
vichyssoise	cold potato soup

WAITERS/WAITRESSES

Waiters and waitresses are people, too, and they deserve to be treated properly.

- When we order, we want to say, "May I please. . . ?"
- When we are served, we want to say "thank you."
- When we have a need, question or a problem, we discreetly call our waiter. This is best done by a hand gesture rather than by voice. Calling aloud may disrupt the entire restaurant. Never get attention by snapping our fingers, clapping our hands or tapping on a glass. If they are close enough to hear you in normal conversational volume, you may say, "Waiter," or "Waitress" and smile.
- When we are finished dining at all but fast-food restaurants, we should leave a "tip" of 15% of the cost of the meal. We want to realize "tips" account for most of the waiter's salary. If he has done an exceptional job, we may tip up to 20% of the meal. If the service was poor, we should still tip, but register a complaint with the manager.

Incidentally, it's wise to check our bill to make certain the "gratuity" hasn't already been added.

No matter how fine the service has been, we don't want to "tip" *twice.*

RESTAURANT NO-NO'S

Never ... **NEVER**

- Blow our straw paper across the room. Remove it with our fingers.

- Blow bubbles with our straw.

- Talk loud and boisterously to disrupt other conversations in the restaurant.

- Play music by rubbing our fingers along the rim of the glass.

- Pick up dishes to assist the busboy in clearing the table.

- Write on cloth tablecloths. This is obviously OK if it is a paper placemat designed for personal artwork.

- Build houses out of sugar packets.

- Pour sugar in the salt shaker.

- Play pranks by unscrewing the lids of salt, pepper, or cheese dispensers.

- Put our elbows on the table.

- If we see a line of people waiting to be seated, we don't want to remain at our table for a leisurely chat after we've finished our meal. If the tables were turned (okay, it's a little pun) we wouldn't enjoy standing in line.

Do We Eat It
With Fork,
Spoon or
Fingers?

Grapes, plums, cherries, celery,
  carrot sticks ....Fingers
Pickles, olives, radishes ....Fingers
Corn on the cob ....Fingers
French fries (fast-food, picnic) ....Fingers
French fries (dining room) ....Fork
Fried chicken (picnic) ....Fingers
Fried chicken (dining room).....................Fork
Watermelon (picnic) ....Fingers
Watermelon (dining room) ....Fork
Strawberries or dessert ....Fork
Cut fruit on dinner plate ....Fork
Dry, crisp bacon ......May be eaten with fingers
Artichoke. ....Dip in butter
Lobster in shell ....Parts can only be eaten
                                               by fingers

Chapter 8

PARTY MANNERS

We may not be "party animals," but we're all invited to parties—birthday parties, graduation parties, weekend parties, lots of different parties.

When parties are fun, we don't even notice the manners that govern our celebration. But when party manners are overlooked, the fun disappears faster than the potato chips. The following guidelines are designed to keep us from some of those embarrassing situations.

INVITATIONS

Every party begins with an invitation. Informal parties are announced by telephone. (All telephone manners learned in Chapter 3 should be used.) When we call, be prepared to give the type of event, and date and time. Be sure to give directions to our home.

More formal parties are announced by written invitation. The written invitation shows forethought.

Again, it should include:
- type of event
- date, time and place

FOR EXAMPLE ...

You Are
Cordially Invited
To A
Birthday Party
For
Mary Doe

7:30pm   *Saturday, May 26, 199?*

2300 Pleasant Place, Town

R.S.V.P.

RSVP: These are four very powerful letters. They're the first letters of four French words which mean, "Respond if you please." In other words, "Call me back as soon as possible to tell me if you are able to attend or not."

When we receive invitations with those four letters, we want to give people the courtesy of replying immediately with our "yes" or "no."

READY OR NOT

Before you arrive at a party, know what to expect. If it's a birthday party, be sure whether or not a gift is appropriate. If so, discover what the guest of honor would enjoy.

If it's overnight, be sure to bring all necessary items, including toothpaste and clean underwear.

ALWAYS BE ON TIME!

Always check on the appropriate dress code.

- casual
- informal
- semiformal
- formal
- costume
- swimwear

*We want to be sure we're
dressed properly for the occasion.*

IT'S
PARTY TIME

*Some people   Others crawl
come alive!   into a shell!*

Well, take heart! The life of the party probably isn't nearly as funny as he thinks he is, and the shrinking violet doesn't need to hide behind a bush. The fact is that no matter what our personality or temperament, there's usually another person present just like us. Look around, find the nearest introvert and have a creative conversation.

Avoid isolating yourself. Interact even if you don't have a pocketful of one-liners. If you're sitting next to a nonstop talker, be a good listener. Good listeners are rare!

Somebody went to a lot of trouble to throw the party. You accepted an invitation. Join in the fun!

A Personal Word
from the author

Parties can turn out differently than we expect.

During my senior year of high school I was invited to a New Year's Eve party. I knew some students in my class were bringing beer, wine and hard alcohol as well as marijuana and cocaine. While I did not drink or do drugs, I knew I would feel the pressure to give in.

When I drove up, I could hear the band playing a block away. Many were smoking. A girl came up to me and asked, "Do you want to go upstairs?" "No," I answered, "everyone is down here." "Yes, I know," she replied, "but I want to go to bed with you."

This is a test, I thought to myself. *I need to pass this test.* So I replied, "I would love to go to bed with you, except I'm a Christian and my body belongs to God. I've already decided I'm not going to do that until I'm married."

Yes, I passed that test but I also learned a difficult lesson. When we go to parties we never know exactly what will happen. We need to be careful that we do not make a stupid decision in a party atmosphere that we would regret later.

IT'S TIME TO GO

- Say a pleasant "Goodnight" to everyone
- Thank our friend and the parents who hosted the party.
- If we'd really like to score points, volunteer to help clean up before we leave.
- If anyone's been drinking at the party, we don't let them drive home. We find a sober driver for them at the party, or we call their parents to pick them up. After all, their parents—and ours too— would rather pick them up at the party than at the hospital.
- It's thoughtful to tell our parents a little bit about the party if possible.

Parents don't care to hear all the details, but they'd like to know if we had a good time at the party.

Chapter 9

DATING MANNERS

"Dating manners?
You must be
kidding! Things like
opening doors for
girls, and stuff like
that! It sounds
old-fashioned
to me!"

A Personal Word
— *from the Author*

When I was dating,
some kids told me that
dating manners were
old-fashioned too. But
that doesn't prove any-
thing ... so are shoes ...
TRUE, a number of gen-
der roles have changed in
our society, but manners are
still the same.

And manners still work for us.

Look at it this way:

We ask a girl out because we like her.
Presumably, we might like another date
too. Now, what's likely to insure a second
date — treating the girl as though she's
special or treating her as if she came in a
grab bag?

The next few pages are for special people.

(GENERAL GUIDELINES)

When we're with a member of the opposite sex, we want to always show respect and consideration.
- Be polite.
- Address each other by name.
- Ask each other's preferences in decisions.
- When asking for a date, don't wait until the last minute. (Part of being considerate.)
- Announce exactly what activity you have in mind. (If you plan to go spelunking, she should have some warning.)

If we don't need to ask the girl's parents permission for the date, plan to arrive 15 minutes early so you can get acquainted with them. *(Be sure to notify your date so you don't catch her in curlers.)* You're showing respect for your date and her parents.
- Find out each other's curfew.
- When we pick up the girl, we're responsible not to keep her out too late. In fact, always aim at 10-15 minutes prior to the deadline. (Bound to score points with parents.)
- Make sure both sets of parents know where you will be and approve of the evening's activity.

A TOUCH OF CLASS

Most anyone can take a girl out on a date. Not everyone can treat her like a lady. We all need a touch of class:

- Open her car door.
- Let her fully seat herself.
- Close her door.

ATTENTION ALL GIRLS:

We want to cooperate with this demonstration of manners. Allow him to show his respect for you this way. (If the young man doesn't open the door for you, loan him this book!)

Make sure the radio volume is at the comfortable level.

• Decide ahead of time who is "buying." Ordinarily the guy buys but "Dutch treating" is more and more acceptable. If the guy invites the girl but intends for her to pay for herself, he needs to invite her to "go Dutch."

• It's always the young woman's choice to refuse a date. There is no need to give any excuse. Simply state, "I'm sorry, I can't go with you Friday night." It's rude for a young man to pursue the issue by asking why. If he does, simply repeat, "I just cannot go, I'm sorry." If the boy gets nasty, ask him, "Would you like to speak with my father about it?" That usually ends the conversation.

• Whenever the other person spends money for your benefit, be sure to express you appreciation.

KINGS: TREAT HER LIKE A QUEEN!

"Ladies"
appreciate
"gentlemen" who:

- Open doors for them.
- Assist them with their coats.
- Help carry their books and packages.
- Permit them to leave an elevator first.
- Carry their open umbrella.

It's not a bad way to be able to walk arm in arm.

All girls love flowers.

They're always appropriate for proms, birthdays and graduations, for example.

And we don't need to spend $50 on a dozen long-stemmed red roses. A hand-picked bunch of daisies or road lilies are fine for low budgets. They won't exactly win first prize in the Rose Bowl Parade, but it's the sentiment that counts, right?

The next time you've got a date — even though it's not a special occasion — be a sport — stop along the road and pick your girl a bouquet. (Be sure to remove the roots.)

WHEN YOU MEET THE PARENTS!

Okay, guys! Now's the time to use all the points we learned in Chapter 1 (Effective Introductions).

Try to relax.

Don't rush the conversation. Be courteous — lots of "sirs" and "ma'ams." If our date is meeting our parents, don't be embarrassed. We need to relax, too, and remember that we're still under our parents' authority. We want to respect them and accept their love and care with appreciation.

CREATIVE IDEAS!

Dating can so easily get in a rut of ...

movies
burgers
mall
more
movies
parking
videos
back to

the mall
another movie
more burgers
blah!!

Everyone enjoys new ideas, like ...

go on a picnic
take a hike together
go for a bike ride
borrow a video camera
and make your own movie
go fishing
sail a boat
plan a cook-out
visit a museum
visit a new church on Sunday
climb a mountain
make a butterfly collection
go horseback riding

You may notice that each of these ideas costs no more than burgers and fries and some of them are free. They will each bring a breath of fresh air into your relationship.

Have fun!

OUR SEXUALITY

The most obvious means of showing disrespect for our date is to violate them sexually or morally. This is an area we must treat with greatest care. It's how headlines are made. As we've said in Chapter 5 on "personal values," our own bodies and certainly the private parts of our bodies are precisely that — private. They should not be exposed to, touched by, or talked about with other people. We want to maintain strict standards so that we don't offend a boyfriend or girlfriend.

When we face the possible temptation to do things we know are wrong, there are a number of approaches we might take.

- Don't date alone; stay in groups of friends.
- Avoid drinking or hanging around students who drink.
- Never be alone together at each other's home. Never, not even baby-sitting.
- Stay physically active — tennis, running, hiking, biking, skiing, swimming.
- Dress modestly.

SINCERE QUESTIONS

1. "What if the guy keeps nagging me to have sex with him?"

Guys who are more interested in your *body* than they are in you will never be satisfied even if you give them what they are asking for. Don't give in to their manipulation. Keep your standards and get rid of the guy. You need a boyfriend who respects you enough to also respect your convictions.

2. "Girls make me nervous. I'm not interested in sex; I just want to get up enough guts to take a girl to a movie. How do I break the ice?"

Start a relationship with girls in a group. After you identify a particular girl you would like to spend an evening with, invite her to a group activity. "Our group is going to the movies Friday night. Would you like to come with me?" Usually, dating is most healthy when it is done in a group anyway.

3. "I don't want to go steady. That makes me nervous. I just want to do things together as friends without getting so serious. Is there anything wrong with that?"

Not at all. In fact, you're wise. Often young men and women who are always going steady are insecure, nervous and possessive. There is no rule of etiquette you are violating by simply dating periodically with no strings attached.

4. "Can I date two guys at one time?"

Yes . . . Just be honest about it to both guys. It's better they learn about it from you than from someone else. If one of the guys gets angry it probably indicates they wanted more of a commitment from the relationship than you were ready to make. If he gets angry, that's his problem, not yours.

5. "I've been dating a guy for two and a half years and lately all we do is fight."

You are probably stale. Most likely someone needs to make a bold decision — you need to open the doors and let in a little fresh air. You need to agree to start dating other people.

6. "I've never gone out on a date and I don't want to."

No problem. You're not weird ... but most likely you'll change your mind someday.

7. "I'd like to date, but I'm just soooo shy!"

Hey, there is probably a girl who looks at you every-day at school and says to herself, "Man, I'd love to have a date with him. I wish someone would introduce us. I'd go up and sit with him in class . . . but . . . but I'm just soooo shy!"
Fifty percent of all people are shy and most of them are also waiting for a date. Just do it.

8. "I like my girlfriend, but her parents drive me crazy."

Look in the mirror and ask yourself,
"Is it possible that I bug her parents too?"

In any event it's tough to show respect for a girl without showing respect for her parents. This doesn't mean parents are perfect. Some parents are difficult to respect. But we don't need to respect them as people; we need to respect their position as parents. Parents don't need to do anything to earn our respect. They've already done the one thing that warrants all the respect necessary. They brought us into the world. Since we owe our existence to them, we can arbitrarily respect their position in our lives.

A Personal Word

- from the Author

A mother of a coed at Clemson University told me recently, "My daughter wanted to go to Daytona Beach, Florida, for spring break. All her friends were going. Then they started reading posters all over campus which read, 'One out of five coeds who go to Daytona Beach for spring break will end up dying from AIDS.' None of them went."

Then the mother added, "My daughter used to be mocked for being a virgin. Now she is glad she is a virgin. In fact, she says she's far more popular because of her standards. She says the guys know they won't catch a disease from her."

Some girls can make a bad decision late on a Saturday night and by Monday morning they have a bad reputation.

Some guys seem to have a one-track mind and appear as though they want to take every girl to bed.

Even though our generation may not always stand up and applaud, students who hold to strict moral standards never need to be ashamed.

SUMMARY

- Be polite at all times.
- Be faithful to honor all curfews.
- Receive not only the girl's permission, but also the girl's parents' permission prior to the first date.
- Use some ol' fashioned class ...
    — Open doors
    — Help on with the coat
    — Hold the umbrella
- Use some creative ideas for dating.
- Maintain a strict moral standard.

Chapter 10

THE BIG PROM
or
GRAD NIGHT

No doubt about it, prom night is one of the biggies of the school year. We can't "fly by the seat of our pants" on this one. It's expensive flying.

Fasten our seatbelts, consider the turbulence below and make a sensible flight plan...

ECONOMY		FIRST CLASS
$50	Tuxedo (man)	$150
$50 (homemade)	Formal (woman)	$500
$15	Corsage/boutoniere	$75
$20	Hair/Make-up	$75
$250	Limo	$750
$25	Dinner before	$125
$25	Prom Tickets	$100
$15	Photographs	$50
$20	After-Party	$600
$15	Accessories	$250
$10	Breakfast	$28
$495	**TOTAL**	**$2,693**

**YOU'RE READY
FOR TAKE OFF!**

PROM DECISIONS

• Our date:

Of all the decisions we face regarding prom night without question the biggest decision is "Who do we go with?" This is somewhat easier for the young man than the young woman, but not much easier. (We'd hate to spend all that money and have a lousy evening.)

- **Color tuxedo and formal:**

Usually it's best for the young woman to make this choice. The young man can always match her if he chooses.

- **Flowers to match:**

Again this must co-ordinate with the young woman's gown.

• **Preprom restaurant:**

Technically this is optional but recently in most areas it's become standard procedure. Whichever restaurant we choose, make our selection as early as possible and make reservations.

• **Prom table:**

Many proms have tables set up around a large ballroom which each seat four to five couples. Again it would be smart to preselect your table so you can be sure to have friends seated with you.

• **Postprom party:**

Next to selecting your date, where you end up following the prom is the second most significant choice you'll make. You need to take into consideration where you and your date's friends are going. If you don't feel comfortable with the options, plan your own party. Again, start planning as early as possible. Both the guy and gal should agree on this important choice.

• **Prom pictures:**

These are almost impossible to avoid. It's an additional expense, but if we refuse it, our girlfriend will think she's a "cheap date." Besides, if we have already spent several hundred dollars, what's another $15-$25?

• **Nonalcoholic:**

Prom night is often the one night all year students get drunk or stoned. If we have convictions, it's best to decide in advance and announce to our date and a small select group of friends that we'll be there to have a great time, but we'll not be drinking alcohol.

• **Price Tag:**

No matter how we add it up, proms are incredibly expensive.

• Rather than spending your parents' life savings or the money you set aside for your college education, we should carefully think through each of the itemized expenses and make sure we stick close to our budget. Also determine in advance who's paying the price tag — we or our parents. Perhaps you can split the cost depending on which items they regard as unnecessary.

Remember ...

All the other manners we've learned apply double for the prom.

- Ask girl's permission; ask parents' permission.
- Be polite.
- Open doors.
- At the table, pull out the chair to seat the girl.
- Maintain strict moral standards, no matter how late at night it *is*.
- Remember all the
table manners ...
    all the
conversation manners ...
    all the
introductions ...

- **BUT DON'T GET UPTIGHT!**
  Don't take yourself too
  seriously! Enjoy your
  date and have fun!

Chapter 11

FAMILY MANNERS

Keeping peace in a large family requires patience, love, understanding and at least two TV sets.

How do you build a family? It's easy! Two people fall in love and get married. How do you maintain the love and the family? Well, for one thing, we can digest this chapter. We all like a good love story.

Manners start in the home. If we "have manners" outside but not inside our homes, we're phonies. Sure, we're with our family members so often we can get sloppy or irritated but we never want to lose our respect or our love for those closest to us.

If we forget our brother's birthday it's only a little thing. If he forgets ours it's a big thing!

We want to turn that perspective around a few times, examine it, and try to look at our family as we'd like them to look at us — in love.

HERE'S A GREAT RECIPE FOR BREAKFAST:

Greet everyone enthusi- astically. "Good morning, Mom. I hope you're feeling well."

"Hi, Dad, hope you slept well last night."

Give everyone a kiss.

Before we leave for school, wish everyone a super day!

When you return from school, observe all the nice things your family does for you:

Say "thank you" for the little things.

"Thank you for doing the laundry."

"Thank you for fixing such a good meal tonight. That was delicious."

"I sure appreciate your working so hard, Dad, so we can live in a nice neighbor- hood."

"Thanks for driving me to Sally's house; I had a great time."

"Thanks for talking to me about my friends; I'm glad you're interested in my life."

We not only have everyone's attention by now, they're probably making long-distance calls to tell the rest of the family about us!

OUR ATTITUDE

We've heard the saying, "Actions speak louder than words." This is true, however ...

... *Attitudes speak louder* than *actions.*

We communicate a great deal with our eyes, our expressions and our tone of voice. If we're angry, frustrated, bored or offended it will certainly be obvious to those who know us best — our parents or brothers and sisters.

It's much easier to change our actions than it is to change our attitudes.

— We still need to try.

• Don't pout.
• Don't withdraw into our own little world.
• Don't talk about how we feel using "I" statements.
    — "I'm frustrated."
    — "I don't blame you, but I admit I'm angry."
    — "I have a problem. I realize everyone else wanted to go birdwatching, but I'm bored."
    — "When you told me you did not like my haircut, I was offended."

Being honest about our attitudes is the only way to help ourselves out of "the pits."

HONESTY . . . THE ONLY POLICY

All communication is based on truth and accuracy. The only basis for relationships is trust and integrity. If one family member ceases to be honest, the family begins to break down.

Lies are born in a variety of situations.
- When we want to seem better than we really are.
- When we want to avoid getting in trouble.
- When we want to get our own way.
- When we are afraid of how people will respond to us.

When parents become suspicious of teenagers, trust begins to break down. Little white lies often grow up to be *baldfaced lies.*

We must realize that the toughest truth is never as fearful an enemy as the softest lie. We must make a commitment: "I will only tell the truth to my family members — even to my parents — and even when it hurts."

"You can fool some of the people all of the time; and you can fool all of the people some of the time; but you can't fool all of the people all the time; and you can't fool God any of the time."

OUR BROTHERS AND SISTERS

We often spend more time with brothers and sisters than with anyone else. This overexposure may cause problems. The following guidelines might solve some of the disagreements.

• Give each other space.

• Don't enter each other's rooms without knocking.

• Don't tease each other.

• Don't "rat" on each other.

• Only borrow with permission and then return promptly.

JUST DO IT

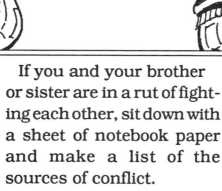

If you and your brother or sister are in a rut of fighting each other, sit down with a sheet of notebook paper and make a list of the sources of conflict.

clothes   bathroom
TV   telephone
music   friends

Try to discuss what you can do about each area in order to avoid conflict. If you can't settle an area, ask your parents for their advice.

FAMILIES DON'T JUST LOVE *BECAUSE* BUT *IN SPITE OF!*

DISGUSTING HABITS

There are many habits we develop which are in themselves harmless. However, when observed daily they tend to drive other people insane ... especially people in our own families. These are best avoided.

- Cracking knuckles
- Loudly passing gas anywhere outside the bathroom
- Staring at people
- Picking nose
- Picking teeth
- Chewing gum with mouth open
- Persistent scalp scratching (like a dog!)
- Vibrating your foot or bouncing your leg up and down nervously
- Spitting

Snorting mucus prior to spitting

THE FIVE BIGGEST DAYS OF THE YEAR

• **Christmas:** Gifts for everyone in your immedaite family (Mom, Dad, brothers, sisters and grandparents) purchased with your own money.

• **Birthdays:** Cards for everyone in your immediate family and gifts for Mom and Dad, brothers and sisters.

• **Mother's Day:** Card and gift.

• **Father's Day:** Card and gift.

• **Anniversary:** Card.

These are days to remember without fail. These are the days on which we show honor to the most important people in our lives.

Never forget the five biggest days!

MISCELLANEOUS

• Always knock before entering anyone else's bedroom or bathroom.

• Always ask permission to borrow clothes, shoes, money, or whatever.

• Lend freely — especially if you intend to borrow.

• Keep a confidence — families share secrets that do not need to be broadcast outside the home.

• Return borrowed items promptly and in good condition. If anything borrowed is broken or stained, it should be fixed as good as new or replaced.

• Give preference to anyone in the family who is sick. Show compassion and kindness.

• Express appreciation. It's easy to get in the rut of taking each other for granted. Don't let it happen. Learn to give sincere compliments.

• Give undivided attention. Be a good listener.

• Use table manners even when it's just family.

• Be respectful of all privileges ...

- time in bathroom
- time in shower
- time on telephone
- volume of our stereo
- choice of TV shows
- use of games

MISCELLANEOUS

• Stand whenever an adult enters the room. This shows honor, respect and preference and should be done for neighbors, relatives, all adults.

• Older brothers and sisters should be protective of younger; both physically as well as morally protective.

• We never interrupt someone's conversation, unless it is an emergency.

• Everyone should care for his own room, keeping it neat and making his own bed.

• Good bathroom manners solve many conflicts before they happen. For example, put away all toothbrushes, combs, etc... Properly rehang all towels. Dry floor and rinse tub after a shower or bath.

(Essentially, it should look the same after it is used as it did prior to use. It should even smell the same! Use air freshener if necessary.)

CHORES

While every student has complained about chores at times, they do have a flip side.

- They teach responsibility.
- They spread the work load around.
- They prepare us to care for ourselves — and to care for others.
- They make us more grateful for all the chores our parents do for us every day.

Every teenager wants privileges, but with each of the privileges comes responsibility. Chores done efficiently and without complaining often convince parents that we're ready to be given more independence.

It is important for every family member to be a contributing family member. Like players on a team, each member needs to pull together so the whole team functions well.

"The dictionary is the only place that success comes before work. Work is the price we must pay for success. I think you can accomplish almost anything if you're willing to pay the price."

Vince Lombardi

REPRESENTATIVES

When we're outside the home, we're representatives of our family. We want people to think highly of our parents and therefore we always want to act in a way that reflects favorably.

In this sense, all manners are family manners. We learn within the home the things that we're to practice outside the home. As we learn to practice respect toward our own family members, we'll find it's much easier to show respect toward new acquaintances. In fact, if we're effective at showing honor to our parents and immediate family, we'll be far more likely to be successful throughout our lives.

If manners are planted in our hearts, they'll be seen in our eyes and heard from our tongues. Our whole family will be in harmony and, before long, the entire community will catch the tune.

Children, obey your parents in the Lord, for this is right. "Honor your father and mother"— which is the first commandment with a promise— "that it may go well with you and that you may enjoy long life on the earth." *Ephesians 6:1-3*

THREE BIG WORDS

Three of the most important words we need to be able to say within our own families are, *"I AM SORRY."* We all make mistakes. We forget instructions. We do things that are wrong. Whether we offend our parents or a brother or sister, when we're wrong we need to admit our error and assume the blame. Rather than trying to publicly defend ourselves, make up excuses, or blame someone else, it makes everything easier to simply admit our mistakes.

THREE OTHER BIG WORDS

There are three other words that sometimes make us feel awkward though they're most important. Parents need to hear them periodically and, even though they may not admit it, brothers and sisters like to hear them also.

About which words are we talking?

I LOVE YOU!

*"Dear friends, let us love one another,
for love comes from God.
Everyone who loves has been born of
God and knows God."*
1 John 4:7

Chapter 12

CAR MANNERS

We can easily see the results of bad manners. They show up in all kinds of embarrassing situations. We can also see the results of bad car manners. They show up in ambulances or hearses.

It's one thing to mess up at a party. It's something else to mess up on the highways.

If *we're* driving, the nicest thing we can do for our pas-  sengers and everyone else on the road is to avoid an accident.

We've learned to respect people. Now we want to learn to respect the two-ton powerhouses we control.

The greatest cause of accidents is the nut that holds the wheel.

BUCKLE UP!

Keep our eyes on the road no matter how pretty the gal next to us might be.

Don't assume the other drivers will do what they're supposed to. (A blinker pointing left doesn't know the driver may be stoned and planning to turn right.)

Speed's a thriller. It's also a killer.

It's better to be *late* in this world than *early* in the next.

The horn is used for safety's sake, not to vent our anger. If someone cuts us off we don't get even we get out of the way, and make certain *we* don't cut someone off.

The driver should obviously be in control of the car. In a real sense, he should also be in control of his passengers.

We don't want any kind of noise or commotion to interfere with our driving concentration.

Safety is the driver's responsibility inside and outside the car. We do whatever's necessary to keep our passengers orderly.

We should consider all traffic regulations. If we read our "Driver's Manual" and drive as it recommends, we should enjoy happy motoring.

PASSENGER MANNERS

When we ride in someone else's car, we want to show our appreciation for their hospitality, and behave like a good guest.

When we enter the car:
- We greet everyone with our famous smile.
- We say hello, using their names.
- We fasten our seatbelts.
- We remain cheerful and cooperative.

When we leave the car, we say "thank you" for the ride.

NEVER RIDE WITH STRANGERS!
NEVER GIVE RIDES TO STRANGERS!

As the saying goes,

Good manners help us to be good passengers with people we know. Good sense tells us *not* to be passengers with people we don't know.

It is one thing to ride with a bad driver; it's worse to ride with a bad person.

Never assume that because the person *looks* trustworthy that they *are* trustworthy. The risks are too high and too obvious.

CAR TRIPS

Spending a great deal of time in a very small space with the same number of people is a test for anyone's manners. Regardless of whether you're traveling with your own family or with a friend, the same guidelines will be helpful.

- Take minimum luggage.
- Bring portable trip games.
- Ask permission to bring a goodie-bag of snack food to share with all passengers.
- Bring enough money.
- Participate in meaningful conversation.
- Keep your arms and legs in your allotted space.
- Be sure to use the bathroom before leaving. If you must stop at a restroom . . . "I'm sorry, but ... please."
- Always thank the driver for the ride.
- If the driver gives permission to snack in the car, make every effort not to spill.
- Volunteer to help with directions. Help read road signs.
- Offer to share in the gasoline expenses.

A car trip is very much like every other part of life's highway. It usually turns out the way we make it.

GETTING YOUR OWN CAR!

Declare a national holiday!!

We're about to get a two-ton shiny badge of maturity!

Of course we're excited! There's a lot to think about.

We want to stay within our budget. By looking through the classified ads in our local newspaper we can often find a good, single-owner used car which will be a great value. Buying new, if we can afford it, has obvious advantages.

• If we're paying for gas, mileage is a very important factor.

• If we're paying for insurance, remember that the more expensive the car, the more expensive the insurance. Also, sports cars are rated far more expensive to insure.

• If we're shopping for a used car we take someone with us who knows what to look for under the hood.

OKAY, DAD'S CAR IS IN THE DRIVEWAY, MY WHEELS ARE IN THE GARAGE!

• Read our automobile owner's manual. While we don't need to be an auto mechanic, it's important to have a general knowledge of our car.

• We should know how to change a tire. If we've never done it before, do it just for practice in our driveway or garage.

• We should also carry in our car a pair of jumper cables in case our battery is dead. They're simple to use and they can save you a great deal of frustration. This is also a helpful way to serve others in their need.

• We should be able to check our own fluid
levels including ...

    - gas
    - oil
    - water
    - water in battery
    - washer fluid
    - brake fluid

• Once a month we should check the air pressure in our
tires and make sure they have proper tire tread.

• Car phones or "bag-phones," which are transferable
from vehicle to vehicle, can provide good security, especially for the young woman driving at night. In case of an
accident or mechanical problem, it provides immediate
access to a familiar voice.

• A car should be washed outside once a week and inside once a month, including dusting and vacuuming. No one should use his car as a locker or a dirty clothes hamper. A car should be kept nearly as clean as a room in our house.

• Always "buckle up" and insist on every passenger using his seatbelt. Don't pull from the driveway until all have cooperated.

> **REMEMBER:**
> A driver's license is not a right to demand
> just because you are the legal age;
> it is a privilege to be earned
> when you show yourself responsible.

The most considerate thing you can do for your car is to avoid an accident.

Good manners promote safety.

A Personal Word
—*from the author*

A car is potentially a lethal weapon. Every year high school students are killed in auto accidents. Certainly not all fatalities are the fault of teenagers, but some are.

No matter how many times you've seen this list before, read it carefully.

- **Do not drink and drive**. Never allow yourself to be driven by a drunk driver.
- **Do not drive late at night if you're exhausted.** If you find yourself dozing off at the wheel, pull over and nap for ten minutes. Resume driving when you are more alert.
- **Do not hot-dog it.** Speed limits save lives. Most traffic fatalities are caused by excessive speeds. Even driving fast for short distances can cause serious accidents.
- **Don't overload your car**, especially the front seat.
- Ordinarily, both hands should be on the wheel.
- As we've said already, **always use seatbelts**.

DRIVING IS A GREAT PRIVILEGE. DO IT RESPONSIBLY.

Happy motoring!

Chapter 13

SUMMER JOBS

Do we need gas money? Clothes? Big date? Saving for college? Maybe a stereo component.

Well, a summer job or a part-time job during the school year is often very attractive. Even if we're loaded and don't need the money (is that possible?) a teenage job offers a great pay-off: discipline, responsibility and experience that's bound to benefit our future.

When we begin our job hunt we want to be sure our manners are showing. For starters, they'll give us confidence that we're putting our best foot forward.

WHERE DO WE START LOOKING?

• Check newspaper ads to see what's available.

• Often high schools have an employment office or a bulletin board that posts opportunities.

• Parents, friends and neighbors will often have personal contacts that will open up opportunities.

• Keep your eyes open for signs advertising "HELP WANTED."

• Knock on a few doors.

There are a large variety of jobs available for students. We can easily think of many more to add to our list:

- store clerk
- fast food
- supermarket
- banks
- baby-sitting
- tutoring
- library assistant
- landscaping
- data processing

- waiter/waitress
- house painting
- yard work
- door-to-door sales
- truck delivery
- secretarial
- day care
- computer programming

Each of these jobs can be helpful in developing our potential.

POTENTIAL:

It's *in* there.
We just have to work it *out!*

A Personal Word

-from the Author

When I was in high school I ran a simple three-day ad in the newspaper:

YARD WORK
Conscientious
high school senior
will do anything.
Call Fred _____.

I received more phone calls then I was able to respond to. I earned $400 per week. I saved most of the money in the bank and when I got engaged four years later I was able to buy my sweetheart a nice diamond ring.

More than earning money, however, summer jobs and part-time jobs teach us responsibility. They teach us the value of money and they challenge us to think ahead and begin planning toward a life career.

WARNING: There is a danger in student jobs. They can easily take our focus off the importance of finishing school, spending time with our families, and working toward long-term career goals. Don't allow part-time or summer employment to side-track you from the truly important things in life.

Perhaps there's a special field we'd like to work in. We might select a few companies in that field and write a letter such as this:

Your name
52 Main Street
Miami, FL 33901

March 22, 1992

Mr. Bob Smith
The Big Company
53 Main Street
Miami, FL 33901

Dear Mr. Smith,

On June 3rd I will be completing my freshman year at Miami High School. I am 15 years old and I am preparing for a career as a corporate secretary. My scholastic average is A-. I am very interested in working for your company as a secretary doing any kind of work. I type 58 words a minute without errors.

I would appreciate the privilege of an interview with you. I am available any weekday after 3:30 p.m. My telephone number is _____ .

Respectfully,
(Signature)

Jane Smart

Be sure to type the letter — ***without errors!***

If you have job experience, a resume is helpful. Keep all the information typed on a single sheet.

Name
Address
Home Phone

Education
Elementary School
High School
(Grade point average)

Job Experience
Most recent listed first

Interests/Achievements
Honors
Awards
Athletics
Career Goals

Personal References
1. Teacher
   Address
   Phone
2. Family Friend
   Address
   Phone

If you line up an interview, be sure to ...

- Arrive at least 15 minutes prior to appointment.
- Dress appropriately — nothing flashy, but clean and neat.
- Smile.
- Use his/her name.
- Use good eye contact.
- Answer questions directly.
- Do not smoke or chew gum during the interview.
- Immediately after the interview, send a brief, though personal, follow-up letter expressing your appreciation for the opportunity to make application. That follow-up letter might be just the edge you need to secure the position.

All the manners we have practiced and learned will pay off in the job interview.

PUZZLE PICTURE:

WHO WILL GET THE JOB?

NOW THAT I HAVE THE JOB

It's important to be a good employee no matter how small or insignificant the job might seem. Here are some helpful guidelines to keep in mind.

- Be loyal — only speak positively about your boss both inside and outside your job.

- Be kind — not only to those above you on the job, but also to those who work *next to* you and those who might even work *under you.*

- Be punctual ... at least five minutes earlier than necessary.

- Be enthusiastic. Don't simply do the minimum; do more than is expected.

- Be humble. Be open to criticism and correction. In fact, it's best to solicit honest criticism. Ask your boss, "Sir (Ma'am), I want to serve you to the best of my potential. If you see anything in my performance that needs improvement, I sincerely want you to let me know."

- Never steal items from work. Certainly don't steal time.

REMEMBER: An honest day's pay for an honest day's work.

• If you don't understand an assignment, it's your responsibility to ask intelligent questions so you'll be able to do a good job. If you don't ask questions and you fail to complete the assignment, it's your fault.

• Most importantly: Listen carefully. Even if you don't like your boss, listen carefully to all assignments.

• Most jobs are teamwork, so get along well with those you work with.

• Say "I'm sorry." We all make mistakes. When we do, these two words can do more to settle the issue than a thousand words of self-justification.

• Do not ask nosy personal questions. This communicates pride and manipulation. We should be modest and expect the same of others.

• Speak clearly. This communicates mental alertness and accuracy.

BABY-SITTING

Baby-sitting is not only one of the most common jobs, it's also one of the most important jobs in the whole world.

When we're asked to baby-sit, we're paid more than a fee — we're paid a compliment! Parents are trusting us with their most valuable possessions — their children.

Parents may not say these words, but when they ask us to baby-sit they're telling us, *You're honest, trustworthy, capable, resourceful, loving, responsible, dependable (and inexpensive!)*. Although baby-sitting is common, we must never take it lightly. It's a special trust.

BEFORE PARENTS LEAVE:

1. Bedtime?

2. Restrictions? Can they play outside? Swimming pool? TV? Snacks?

3. Assignments? Homework? Chores?

4. Infant's special needs: Bottle? Diapers?

5. Where are parents going? Name, address, phone?

6. In case of emergency: Street address, 911, doctor?

7. Receive special permission: to use the phone, have a friend over, eat food or drink beverage.

8. What time will parents return?

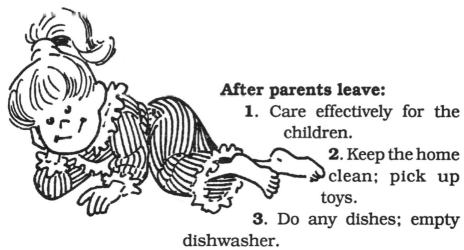

After parents leave:

1. Care effectively for the children.

2. Keep the home clean; pick up toys.

3. Do any dishes; empty dishwasher.

4. Take phone messages including time, person, phone number, purpose of call. It is safest not to announce that you are the baby-sitter. For security reasons simply say, "They are not able to come to the phone right now. May I have them call you later?"

5. Honor parents' restrictions including children's bedtime. If the child stubbornly refuses to obey your curfew, don't use physical discipline and don't allow yourself to become angry. If the child doesn't cooperate with your instructions simply report them to the parents when they return. It's the children's responsibility to obey the baby-sitter. It's the responsibility of the baby-sitter to report them to the parents when they don't.

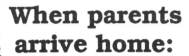

When parents arrive home:

1. Greet them with a smile. "Did you have a good time?"
2. Report phone calls.
3. Report children's behavior and bedtime.

BABY-SITTING FEE:

Baby-sitting is usually paid on an hourly rate and differs according to the number of children, age of the baby-sitter and demand.

• Always settle the rate prior to the baby-sitting assignment. This will avoid either parent or baby-sitter being disappointed.

• Also understand who provides transportation and the hours your service is required. You want to avoid surprises.

Chapter 14

LETTERS & CORRESPONDENCE

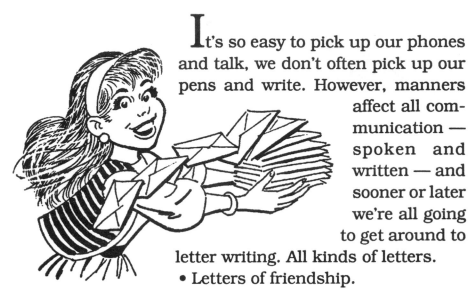

It's so easy to pick up our phones and talk, we don't often pick up our pens and write. However, manners affect all communication — spoken and written — and sooner or later we're all going to get around to letter writing. All kinds of letters.

- Letters of friendship.
- Letters of "thanks" for gifts and special acts of kindness.
- Letters of appeal.
- Letters of recommendation.
- Letters of congratulations.
- Letters of compassion.
- Letters for business.

Some letters are very business-like. Some are VERY personal.

WHEN ARE LETTERS APPROPRIATE?

- Whenever gifts are received, a note should be handwritten within one week.
- When family members celebrate birthdays or anniversaries, a card or note should be sent.
- When someone has done a special service for us, our appreciation should be expressed in writing. If a "thank you" is worth verbalizing, at times it also needs to be written.
- When someone close to us achieves a level of success, a letter of encouragement is always fitting.
- When someone close to us suffers a severe loss, such as a death in the family, a letter of condolence is appropriate.

This latter kind of letter isn't easy to write, because — *let's face it* — we're all inclined to avoid tough subjects. We feel our attempts to express ourselves might seem awkward or inadequate.

But, again, manners come to our rescue. The act of showing compassion, friendship, and love speaks much louder than our words.

In short, don't stew over *how* to do it — just *do* it.

OTHER GUIDELINES

- If our letter contains more than a single page, begin the second page on another sheet of paper and number the second and all additional pages.
- If the letter is to a personal friend or family member for non-business purposes, it should be handwritten.
- If it is for business purposes or to someone outside our family or circle of friends, it should be typed.
- If it is handwritten, after the second page, it should be written front and back. The first sheet should always be written on only one side.

- If you have printed stationery with personalized letterhead, the first sheet should always have the letterhead. All other sheets within the letter should be without letterhead.

- Whatever we put in writing may be read and reread by more than the single intended recipient. We want to be courteous in expressing ourselves particularly if we are issuing a complaint. Even a "love letter" might put on paper things we someday regret. Just a warning.

It's wiser to choose what we say than to say what we choose.

THE STANDARD LETTER

My name
My address
Today's date

Dear friend,

This letter is following the standard form of a letter with my name, address, and today's date in the top right-hand corner. The body of the letter continues using proper margins on both right- and left-hand sides.

Respectfully (*or whichever closing you choose*),

Your signature

THE FORMAL LETTER

My name
My address
Today's date

Their name
Their address

Dear Mr. Fuffufnick,

I appreciate the free trip you gave me to Hawaii last month. That was most generous. I was happy to feed your cat while you were out of town for the weekend. I would be happy to serve you again.

Most sincerely,

Personal signature
My name (typed)

Again . . .

- Use proper margins on both sides
- Use whichever closing you choose
- Sign your name above your typed name

KEEP THOSE
THANK-YOU NOTES COMING!

If we're not thankful for what we've got, we're not likely to be thankful for what we're going to get. In other words, if we don't express thanks for a gift we get, we may not get more gifts.

We all receive special gifts of love that deserve a special response:

- Christmas or birthday gift from someone out of state or across town.
- Any money gift or other gift sent through the mail.
- A special favor.
- An overnight visit.
- A dinner party or luncheon.
- A special event.

Thank-you notes are available in many stores. We can even create our own for a personal touch. Simply fold a plain piece of paper both ways and use your imagination.

SAMPLE THANK-YOU NOTES

Today's date
Dear Grandma and Grandpa,

It was so thoughtful of you to give me a brand-new BMW for my graduation. Red is my favorite color. I will take good care of it.

You are special to me.

Love, Fred

P.S. My friends like the car too.

Today's date

Dear Mrs. Jones,

Thank you for letting me stay with you in your vacation home in Daytona Beach over spring break. I had a wonderful time. I hope to do it again sometime.

Respectfully,

Fred Hartley

SUMMARY

- We want our personal letters or notes to be handwritten.
- Our business or formal letters should be typed, using proper margins, and proper spacing.
- Our thank-you notes should be sent within one week when a gift is received through the mail.
- Whatever we put in writing can be read and reread by other people besides the intended recipient. We want to be careful what we write ... it might come back and embarrass us if we 're not careful.

By the time we've read this far, our manners are bound to be reflected in the way we treat others. We're probably noticing that others are treating us in new and special ways too. Take note of these special acts of friendship ... send a *thank-you* note. Tell your friends you appreciate them.

Chapter 15

GUEST MANNERS

*When we're a guest, we bring a minimum of
gear and a maximum of manners.*

Puzzle Picture:
          Find the guy who has it backwards.

The welcome mat is out. Step on it! Wipe our feet for a clean start! We want to have a good visit. Our hosts do too!

It's their house, not ours. Their TV set, their fridge. We don't push buttons and open doors as freely as we do at home, but we can have fun and have respect too.

• We remember our smile, eye contact and pleasant conversation.

• We interact comfortably with our friend's parents. Use their names.

"That's an interesting story, Mr. Snyder."

- Always hang up our clothes.
- Knock before opening closed doors.
- Depend on our host to clue us in on:
    Where we sleep
    Breakfast time
    Curfew
    Any special household rules.
- Show appreciation for the hospitality and all meals. Verbalize our feelings.
- Special item: Don't handle bric-a-brac. (We might shatter an heirloom and a friendship!)

- We always ask permission to use the phone. (Don't put long-distance calls on our host's bill.)
- Keep the bathroom neat.
- Avoid long-distance, record-setting showers.
- Leave towels folded neatly and without our fingerprints.
- Make our bed. (C'mon, you can do it!)
- Keep noise levels considerate.
- Become a volunteer. Offer to help clean table, for example.

If Our Host Has A Pool

Be careful!
Here's where we can really get in over our heads.

I t's fun getting into a pool. It's no fun getting into hot water. We want to keep our energy and enthusiasm under control.

- Running around the pool is dangerous.
- Pushing people in the pool is dangerous.
- We don't take food or drink into the pool.
- Be sure we know all pool rules and obey them.
- Think ahead. The pool is definitely not the bathroom.
- We don't enter house dripping wet.
- When our suits are wet, we don't sit on any furniture except "outdoor furniture."

Pool rules, like all household rules, aren't designed to throw water on our fun. They're meant to *guarantee* a good time by avoiding an accident, a fight or worse. They're really for *everyone's* benefit.

So we put our manners into practice and have a great visit. And when friends come to visit us, we appreciate *their* manners. And that's the whole idea of manners — they work *both* ways.

Chapter 16

SCHOOL MANNERS

I WILL NOT BRING MY BOOM BOX
   TO SCHOOL.

I WILL NOT PARK IN THE
   PRINCIPAL'S PLACE.

I WILL NOT MEET DEBBIE IN THE
   LIBRARY ROMANCE SECTION.

I PROBABLY WON'T GRADUATE,
   EITHER!

Despite the behavior of some students, there's a big difference between the classroom and the playground.

The primary purpose of school is education, not entertainment. Of course learning should be exciting and it can be fun. It's important, however, as we grow up to learn to identify the things that help us mature and the things that don't.

We want to focus on the things that work in the classroom and the things that don't.

THE FACTS OF LIFE

Our teachers are in charge! They assign homework, give grades, privileges, detentions, time-outs and — yes — graduation diplomas.

We don't have to be on the honor roll to understand the importance of a good relationship with our teachers.

Good manners don't allow apple polishing but they certainly avoid the pits!

- Our teachers deserve our respect and attention.
- We want to take down all assignments accurately.
- We greet our teachers each day by name. If they have a doctorate, we use it. "Good morning, Dr. Sweet."
- We don't hesitate to ask a question if something isn't clear to us.
- Some students study enough to *survive*. We study enough to *thrive*.
- We're not reluctant to do *more* than is expected of us. Our teachers want to touch our lives. It's up to us whether their touch is a pat on the back or a rap on the knuckles.

LET'S LOOK
AT OUR CLASSMATES

W e're not responsible for our classmates. We're responsible to them. It's our class, and we've got a lot in common. Take a second look at our classmates. Obviously, we don't have the same looks, talents or personalities because we're each unique. That's why it's ignorant to joke about differences rather than respect them.

In the same spirit, we don't want to laugh at a classmate's goof or make fun of a "dumb" answer. We want to be a positive influence in our class.

- Assist a struggling student.
- Be a peacemaker.
- Get involved in projects and class discussions.
- Set the best possible example.

CHEATING

Cheating is a sneaky habit. It sort of crawls in the back door and does its dirty work without being noticed — usually. That's how cheating starts. Actually, we're not cheating the teacher; we're cheating ourselves.

Some students justify their cheating:

- **Fear of failure.**
- **Forgetting an assignment.**
- **Laziness** — *it's easier than studying*
- **Necessity** — *"I'll flunk if I don't!"*

Cheating has consequences. Our prisons are full of them. Cheating is a form of stealing and lying. It's bound to make us feel guilty. It establishes a very destructive pattern. It prevents us from becoming mature adults because it's an effort to avoid assuming responsibility for our own actions. It's weakness at its worst. **It cheats us** of our own ability! Cheating is really like a fisk hook — it's much easier to get caught than uncaught.

HOW TO MAKE
THE GRADE

> School is a building with four walls and tomorrows inside!
>
> We don't want to leave school without getting the most out of it any more than we want to go through life without living it.

So we give it our best shot.

- We pay attention. Take notes. Exercise our brains in class discussions.
- Do our homework. There's a good reason for it. Don't leave major projects until the last minute.
- Reading effectively isn't an option; it's a necessity.

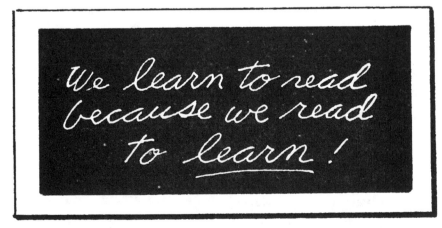

We learn to read because we read to learn!

An education isn't something we've had; it's something we're always getting.

Chapter 17

CHURCH MANNERS

Good manners:
Invite a friend to church
Bad manners:
If they decline, drag them!

We've all noticed that there are many types of churches that have different kinds of services and all sorts of people inside.

However, there's only one God.

We know that manners affect our relationship with people. Church manners affect our relationship with God. Sounds heavy, doesn't it? And yet God wants us to be comfortable about church. It's His house and He wants us

to feel right at home. *So relax.* Sense His acceptance. He loves us and He's the author of manners.

We're not too good to stay away from church and we're not too bad to go in.

Sitting in church, we notice that not everyone is focused on God. For example:

"Kim's wearing the outfit that was on sale last week."

"Ted's sitting with Sally. They just don't seem right for each other."

"Oh, brother! I can't believe we're singing hymn 287 again!"

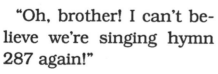

It's much better to see things through God's eyes, isn't it? He's got the best perspective. He told us to love each other; to forgive and to help one another; to turn the other cheek and to go the second mile.

Pretty practical manners, aren't they? It's easy to see what this kind of behavior can do for our relationships — not just in church, but in our homes, our schools and on our streets and sidewalks.

We quickly learn that while church manners show our respect for God's sovereignty they also do a lot for us. After all, God's got it all together. We're the ones who need all the help we can get to solve life's mysteries and get through the dark spots.

We can understand our fear of the dark, but why are we afraid of the light?

"Do not let your hearts be troubled. Trust in God."
John 14:1

Oh sure! It's easy to "sing it" and "pray it" in church. How do we "live it" when we're tired of trying to rise above hurts and disappointments?

Faith is continuing to run the race when we're exhausted, knowing we'll get a second wind.

He gives us second wind for the second mile.

We discover that the highest form of manners take hold in our lives when we simply act out — *in God's grace* — the words we sing and pray and read in church. Word like:

- **Love**
- **Joy**
- **Peace**
- **Patience**
- **Kindness**
- **Goodness**
- **Faithfulness**
- **Gentleness**
- **Self-control**

God is the perfect gentleman. We want to get to know Him in a very *personal* way and share Him in a very *practical* way. That's what His church is all about. That's what manners are all about too.

God wants us to keep in touch so He can help us to grow and mature. He knows that life is sort of like riding a bike — you don't fall unless you stop pedaling.

God even gave us His phone number to emphasize that He's always available: **Jeremiah 33:3** — *"Call to me and I will answer you and tell you great and unsearchable things you do not know."*

OH, C'MON! I don't have to go to church. I can watch it on TV!

The difference between going to church and watching it on TV is similar to the difference between calling your girl on the phone and having a date with her! There's nothing like getting involved!

We have all kinds of opportunities for involvement at church:

- Sunday school
- Choir
- Youth groups
- Help out in kitchen
- Write a letter to a missionary (and get one in return)
- Fill in your own ideas _____

- Help out in office
- Offer car rides
- Weekend camping
- Pray for others

At church we can be part of something much bigger than ourselves. God's love is more than just the basis for all manners. It's where we find ourselves, our purpose and all the exciting discoveries awaiting us in the life He gives.

Remember your Creator in the days of your youth.
Ecclesiastes 12:1a

Before we leave church, let's look at the sum total of all manners — The Golden Rule. **Do to others as you would have them do to you.** *(Luke 6:31)*

It's easy for us to remember this good advice. It's not quite as easy to apply it at all times. That's when it's good to remember the other things we've learned in church. We have help.

Now let's go out there and enjoy the great adventure of life together.

> **"Love each other as I have loved you."**
> *John 15:12*